ALIENATION AND FREEDOM

ALIENATION AND FREEDOM

Richard Schmitt

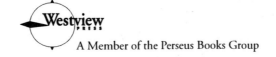

A Member of the Perseus Books Group

Copyright © 2003 by Westview Press, A Member of the Perseus Books Group

Westview Press books are available at special discounts for bulk purchases in the United States by corporations, institutions, and other organizations. For more information, please contact the Special Markets Department at the Perseus Books Group, 11 Cambridge Center, Cambridge, MA 02142, or call (617) 252-5298.

Published in 2003 in the United States of America by Westview Press, 5500 Central Avenue, Boulder, Colorado 80301-2877, and in the United Kingdom by Westview Press, 12 Hid's Copse Road, Cumnor Hill, Oxford OX2 9JJ

Find us on the World Wide Web at www.westviewpress.com
A Cataloging-in-Publication data record for this book is available from the Library of Congress.

ISBN 0-8133-6588-0 (hc), 0-8133-2853-5 (pbk)

CONTENTS

PREFACE

I wrote this book primarily for students, but professional philosophers will profit from reading it because the concept of alienation has been little discussed in the professional philosophy of the last twenty or more years. This neglect is justified by the excessive abstractness of previous treatments of alienation, as well as by the fact that these treatments are far more tightly connected to the Marxian tradition than they should be. In this book, Marx is important but he is no longer the fount of all wisdom with respect to alienation. I have also made major efforts to render the discussion of alienation much more concrete. Since philosophy is by its very nature quite abstract, I have made good use of the contributions of various novelists who give us a much more detailed and therefore much more persuasive picture of the alienated life.

Discussions of alienation tend in two opposite directions. On the one hand, we have many summaries of Marx's writings that list the four conditions of alienation found in Marx's early essay "Alienated Labor" (the worker is separated from the work process and its product, from his fellow workers, and from the nature he shares with other human beings). To this many writers add a summary of Marx's observations in *Capital* (in the section bearing the title "The Fetishism of Commodities"), where he claims that capitalism confuses us about our power to change the social system. Such restatements of Marx characterize some pervasive social conditions that constitute one aspect of alienation. On the other hand, writers about alienation focus on the subjective experience of alienation. Often those accounts are associated with the existentialists, who tell us a great deal about lives that feel empty, without meaning or direction, and about human beings who are depressed, aimless, and unhappy. Thus alienation is often discussed either as a set of social structures or, equally frequently, as a range of pervasive emotions.

If you read him carefully, Marx turns out to have included both aspects in his account of alienation. He tells us not only about the social condition of the worker but also about how the worker feels:

> He does not fulfill himself in his work but denies himself, has a feeling of misery rather than well-being, does not develop freely in his mental and physical energies but is physically exhausted and mentally debased. The worker, therefore, feels himself at home only during his leisure time, whereas at work he feels homeless. His work is not voluntary but imposed, forced labor. It is not the satisfaction of a need, but only a means for satisfying other needs. . . . It is not his own work but work for someone else. . . . [I]n his work he does not belong to himself but to another person. (Marx 1963:125; emphasis in original)

Marx's account of alienation includes both the structure of the worker's situation and the emotions that structure evokes. But it includes more as well. It tells us that the structure is not of the worker's making, and that the emotions with which we respond to those structures are only barely under our control. Discussions that are limited to the social structures of alienation and the emotional repercussions of those structures focus on human subjects as mainly passive, shaped by social conditions, and overcome by negative emotions. Such accounts ignore the effects on human beings' active conduct of their own lives. Indeed, they ignore the most important part of any adequate discussion of alienation: the ways in which alienation affects and distorts the way we live our lives. Alienation, properly understood, is manifest in our lives insofar as we are active in living them.

Human beings act. Marx expresses that fact by placing work at the center of human life. Alienation is a grave injury because it hinders and distorts our activities. It limits the scope of our lives. The alienated worker, Marx says, "does not develop freely in his mental and physical energies": His range of possible lives is very limited because he is "physically exhausted and mentally debased." Thus the many different ways in which human activities are restricted and impoverished by alienation are the centerpiece of any useful discussion of that condition.

An account of alienation that omits any of these aspects is incomplete. Oppressive social conditions do not always alienate. In some cases, groups emerge from domination by foreign occupation or by ruthless governments with their pride and energy unscathed. Their suffering does not affect the integrity of their members or the vigor with which they live their lives. In other cases, oppressive conditions elicit heroic acts of resistance that no one could have expected, challenging persons to assume new and extraordinary dimensions. In that respect they are very different from the alienated, who "come to doubt that they have the capacity to do the sorts of things that only persons can do, to be what persons, in the fullest sense of the term, can be" (Bartky 1990:29). As long as oppression spawns resistance, the personality of the oppressed remains intact. Oppressive conditions alienate only when they transform the personality. Energy becomes depleted by continued struggles, and resistance weakens. Lives become crabbed; enthusiasm wanes and is replaced by a persistent low level of discouragement, the expectation that things will turn out badly. Enterprise is limited, hope feeble; one sticks to the familiar and does not strike out in unaccustomed directions. Human relations are not altogether satisfactory for reasons no one understands. Life is all right but not really good.

Describing oppressive structures falls short of describing alienation. Oppression and alienation need to be distinguished. Oppression restricts one's freedoms and rights; alienation attacks one's personality. In favorable cases, oppression goads us into resistance and thereby strengthens our person. Alienation has the opposite effect. It weakens us, making us less able to resist oppression.

But, similarly, stories about unhappiness in its various forms often have little to do with alienation. Unhappiness is not always a sign of alienation. There is a great deal of sorrow in this world, not all of it the concomitant of alienation. Those who experience oppression, deprivation, or great losses feel pain and bitterness but often recover from their intense suffering and emerge into a more serene state of mind with their powers enhanced and their understanding sharpened. They are alienated only if bitterness corrodes their souls so that they give up living their lives thoughtfully, just taking what comes, with few complaints and little joy. The alienated are sometimes unhappy and sometimes not. Unhappiness is not the exclusive symptom of alienation.

Many writers about alienation have ignored its central characteristics—that it deforms our personalities and makes our lives less firmly ours, less adventurous, and less meaningful. For this reason I have made a considerable effort in this book to provide detailed descriptions of how lives are narrowed by alienation. After introducing the concept of alienation in Chapter 1 by citing some literary examples of it, I present this concept—the failure to make one's life one's own—in Chapter 2 as elaborated by some of the most profound thinkers about alienation. In the same chapter, readers will encounter some alternative views on alienation that the more detailed systematic account of alienated lives in Chapter 3 shows to be misguided. Human personalities are quite varied, and humans live under very different conditions. Accordingly, this chapter shows that the deformation of personality, characteristic of alienation, takes many different forms. Prevailing conceptions of alienation often oversimplify. In Chapter 4, having established a fairly detailed understanding of alienation, I discuss the social conditions that aggravate alienation. Finally, Chapter 5 shows that freedom is limited for the alienated because they are unable to use the liberties they have; their lives are too circumscribed, too timid, and too disjointed for that.

A number of good friends have read all or parts of the original manuscript. I am indebted to Anatol Anton, Murray Code, Roger Gottlieb, Amelie Rorty, Annie Smith, and David Williams for reading this manuscript in various stages and making extremely helpful and insightful suggestions. The anonymous reviewer for the publisher also gave helpful advice for improving the book. The librarians at Holy Cross generously allowed me access to their library's resources. I dedicate the book to my life partner Lucy Candib and to my children Addie Candib and Eli Schmitt. All three contributed significantly to this work, not only by reading drafts and making concrete suggestions but also by sharing with me an outlook on the world that takes alienation very seriously, and is critical of our society for fostering it.

                                                                                                    R. S.

ALIENATION AND FREEDOM

Alienation

Friends alienate their friends by being unexpectedly cold and distant; politicians alienate their constituents when they support legislation to benefit large donors instead of ordinary citizens; husbands alienate their wives by having affairs. Alienation arises when relations falter, when distrust separates persons who had earlier understood and trusted each other. Conversations become guarded and formal; feelings are concealed instead of being shared. One transfers one's trust to other persons and perhaps even begins to malign those whom one had earlier defended warmly. Alienation, then, often refers to a growing estrangement between individual persons, to cooling affections, and to a loss of trust.

This estrangement is, to begin with, a matter of feeling: We feel alienated from someone, we say, because we no longer trust a former friend, we do not feel comfortable with him. Perhaps we don't like him any more, or are bored with him; he seems different. But alienation also affects our understanding. I feel alienated from my onetime friend because I no longer understand him. Our lives have taken different paths; I no longer share his interests and enthusiasms, and since we do different things in our lives, much of the time I do not know exactly what he is up to. I do not understand why an intelligent person should hold the views he defends; his interests seem trivial and his goals reprehensible. I no longer recognize in him, or in his opinions, the friend I once treasured.

This estrangement also has an active component. Friendship extends one's powers. If you ask friends a favor, they try to respond. They make efforts to please; your opinions carry weight with them. But I have no influence on the former friend who is now a stranger. I can't do anything with him, and if I asked him a favor he would refuse. Nor will he listen to me because my opinions seem to him as outlandish as his sound to me. Neither of us will consider the other's ideas seriously, let alone act on them.

Estrangement brings with it a loss of power—an incapacity to have any influence on the onetime friend.

This is alienation from one or two persons. But often we speak of being alienated from larger groups. The friends from high school seem different when I return home from college; they seem less interesting. The old intimacy has evaporated and we do not know what to talk about. My church has many new members whom I do not know, and the new minister is preoccupied with social concerns that do not interest me. I go to services less frequently and don't have much to say to other parishioners after the service. I feel strange in what was once a comfortable place. New management at work has replaced the old supervisors and work rules; there is a new spirit of dogged devotion to work that makes work less pleasant. Some of my oldest friends have left. Their replacements have a different outlook on the world and I feel uncomfortable with them. Relations at work are not as comfortable as they once were. Here alienation separates me from a whole group.

Wider in scope is the alienation of the expatriate who moves abroad because the customs and preoccupations of his fellow citizens differ from his own. They do not value what is of paramount importance to him. Their daily preoccupations, their conversations, their enthusiasms and prejudices grate on him. Many American writers moved to France between the great wars because they felt stifled by the pervasive anti-intellectualism at home. African-American artists could not flourish in a racist society that excluded, ignored, and, worse, devalued them. Alienated from their own society, they fled to another country where, even though strangers, they could feel more at home. For many young people, the world of their parents, or of school, is similarly alien territory. They meet only criticism and disapproval from adults whose concern seems to them opaque at best and ridiculous at worst. If only they could escape!

Alienation comes between us and other individuals, or groups, or entire societies; but it also distances us from our own life. If one never feels completely at ease or in control at work, in friendship or love, and in one's own body, one is alienated from one's life or, as we also say, from oneself. Never quite sure why one is here, or whether this is the right place to be, one is unable to still the questions of whether one ought perhaps to be somewhere else or doing something quite different. One fears having some terrible hidden defect; if only one were different, everything would be all right. Life seems utterly accidental; it unfolds but without rhyme or reason, unpredictable and subject to sudden unexpected change. Franz Kafka (1952) illustrates this radically opaque life in his story about Gregor Samsa, who wakes up one morning to find himself transformed into a giant cock-roach. A traveling salesman working for a tyrannical boss, whose demands and tantrums are as unintelligible as they are unpredictable, he spends his evenings at home, with his parents and sister, in a life of stifling monotony. Nothing makes sense in this life because it is not under Gregor's control or shaped by his choices. Hence, discovering that he has become a cockroach is no more exceptional than what he experiences every day. When noth-ing makes any sense, even the most extraordinary event is commonplace.

This is alienation in its fullest sense. In all areas of life one feels oneself superfluous. "I am unwanted, *de trop*," says a character in one of Sartre's novels (Sartre 1964:164).

> Those people laughing over there—I think they must be each other's friends and they remind me that I have no friends to laugh with. The animated conversation at the lunch table makes me feel dull and excluded. In meetings, I am overcome with irrational anger at everyone. At home, the rest of the family seems to share secret un-derstandings which I am not part of. The day's news seems to be from a different planet—it rarely has anything to do with me and my life, and where it does impinge on me I am utterly powerless to change anything. I would not know who to talk to, and if I did, they would not pay any attention to me.

Simple alienation from specific persons or groups plays a very different role in one's life from that of the global alienation that affects every aspect of one's existence. Simple alienation is caused by specific actions or events: When my friend forgets to invite me to his birthday party, which I have at-tended in many previous years, it signals a rift that has been developing for a long time, whether that slight is intentional or just an oversight. When a young man hears only daily demands to clean his room, reminders to do his homework, or questions as to why his clothes have to be as outlandish as they appear to his parents, he feels unloved and distances himself. But not all of his relations are doomed to be cold. He can find other adults from whom he can take advice, hear praise, and receive affectionate support. Simple alienation follows specific events, and it is specific: Distanced from some persons or groups, one remains free to find other nourishing relations. But global alienation poisons the atmosphere everywhere. Nowhere are there sharp edges; everything is difficult to see clearly. No situation is plain; all are full of mystery and incomprehension. I appear to be a stranger to everyone; all others participate in a life that I can glimpse but not really see clearly, let alone share. Kept apart by an invisible wall, I am all alone in ways I cannot even articulate and for reasons I cannot begin to grasp.

This global alienation brings with it global disabilities. The world is unintelligible to me: I do not understand what other people are up to or what they expect of me. I would like to make friends and find lovers but am too clumsy to approach them. It is difficult to understand who likes me and who does not and to interpret what others say to me. In many ways I do not understand myself. I find myself getting enraged without quite knowing what about. I feel anxious, when there seems no provocation, and exuberant, when this day is no different from other days. Unable to understand myself, or the world around me, I do not know where I am going or what a good life might be for me. My life lacks direction; it is without guiding projects. Even worse, were I to make plans I would lack the power to execute them. I cannot get others to attend to me and to take my work or my opinions seriously. In a world that is impenetrable to me, I am without power. My life is not my own.

A life that is not my own, that I do not understand, that does not realize my plans or fulfill my desires, is not worth a great deal. It is an utter disappointment; one can only withdraw into irritable sadness. Global alienation devalues life. It is behind the pervasive despair that Nietzsche called *nihilism*.

Global alienation is therefore often grim, as if groping in a permanent damp fog; but it does not need to be oppressive. One can relieve the isolation by making friends with one and all, the person in the next seat on the bus or the nice couple in the house next door. After they move away, the new neighbors become just as good friends overnight. If things make little sense, they can at least be pleasant, and rather than be bored one can go out and distract oneself, or watch the wonders of the world on television. One can feel vicariously powerful by watching the fights during ice hockey games, or cheering on your man in a wrestling match. One can find instant community in chat-rooms or respite in drugs. If the world seems full of nameless danger, one can carry a gun. Weapons or powerful cars contradict one's knowledge that one can do or is nothing. One need not allow alienation to cause one pain if one can conceal it, divert oneself, or make do with what there is today—now. One is not really in this life but is more like a spectator, being entertained and distracted by what happens day after day.

Yes, this life is happening to me; to the person with this body and this history. But I blundered into it rather than choosing it; nor have I made many efforts to shape it in one direction or another. I have few goals and barely think about my life as a whole. It just flows along—pleasantly at best but sometimes just a familiar round of work and leisure.

Alienation is not always bathed in gloom. Nor are all sad, discouraged lives alienated. Suffering has many sources other than alienation. Lives lived deliberately and without self-deception are likely to contain acute suffering that one cannot evade because one tries to live without deceiving or distracting oneself. Although alienated lives are often shallow, intent only on avoiding all unpleasantness, if one lives life fully one will have to experience its pain more acutely than the alienated often do. Alienation should not be confused with sadness or depression; unhappiness is not the most ordinary and frequent symptom of alienation.

In different situations alienation has a very different scope. On the one hand, there is very specific alienation, such as having a falling-out with a friend that may last for just a short time. On the other hand, there is global alienation—the experience of persons whose life seems without meaning, who lack a definite identity, who have no reasons for their actions. The global alienation that disturbs one's entire life is our topic here. The difference between specific and global alienation is of some importance; it is discussed at the beginning of this book because the two are often confused. Readers should be sure to keep in mind that it is global alienation we are concerned with. As we discuss alienation, do not think about momentary estrangements between persons or situations; rather, understand that we are talking about entire lives that make no sense, and about persons who are deeply bewildered about who they are and where they are going. At different times of one's life, alienation obviously looks different. Older persons can look back on their life and wonder about its continuities and discontinuities and about the ways in which they managed and the ways in which they failed to give some coherence and meaning to it. For a young person, questions about alienation arise in the context of a life just starting; they are questions about what to do in one's life, what will be important, what will be worth fighting for, and what mere distractions.

Human lives are as different as the persons living them. Generalities about alienation may well not apply precisely to anyone's life because alienation takes many different forms. Some specific examples will illustrate this.

The hero of Leo Tolstoy's *The Death of Ivan Ilych* is the son of prosperous civil servants. He attends law school and then goes into government service as a prosecutor. He is

an intelligent, polished, lively, agreeable man . . . a capable, cheerful,
good-natured, and sociable man though strict in the fulfillment of
what he considered his duty: and he considered his duty to be what
was considered so by those in authority. Neither as a boy nor as a
man was he a toady, but from early youth was attracted to persons of
high station . . . assimilating their ways and views of life and establishing friendly relations with them. (Tolstoy, 1960:105)

Because he grew up in a milieu of public servants, he goes to law school to
prepare himself for a civil service career. He adopts the manners and beliefs
of his surroundings, moderated to some extent by his innate good nature.
He is probably a kinder prosecutor than some others because he is a well-
intentioned person. He does not abuse his power but, rather, tries to soften
its effects. ". . . [O]n the whole his life ran its course as he believed life
should do: easily, pleasantly and decorously" (p. 117). But without thinking, he derives his ideas on how to live, on how to spend his time and energy, from the persons among whom he finds himself. How he lives is
mostly determined by the accidents of his birth.

He marries in good time and has a daughter and a son. His marriage is
only a moderate success because periods of amorous harmony alternate
with long stretches of bitter conflict. His relations with his children are ordinary and mostly distant, as are those of other fathers in his set. In this respect, as in all others, his life conforms to convention.

When he secures a better job, he buys a house in the new city and gets
deeply involved in furnishing it. One day, while standing on a ladder, he
falls, hitting his hip on the finial of a curtain rod. Not seriously hurt, he
congratulates himself on being sufficiently nimble to land on his feet. But
the bruise on his hip does not go away; he has more pain. He sees a doctor
who is obviously baffled by his condition. Panicked, Ivan Ilych sees other
doctors whose stories and medicines are different but no more effective.
His illness turns very serious. All the while, his family withdraws and so do
his friends. Eventually, "the whole interest he had for other people was
whether he would soon vacate his place, and at last release the living from
the discomfort caused by his presence and be himself released from his suf-
ferings" (pp. 134–135).

He is terribly sad and frightened. But no one will comfort him; no one is
willing to admit that he is, in fact, dying because doing so would just make
everyone else fear for their own life. He is in despair because he does not
want to die. He wants to live. But then he asks himself: Live how? In the
face of death, in the face of the realization that life is limited, he wonders

whether he has lived his life as well as he might have. He has lived his life as he has wanted to, "easily, pleasantly and decorously." But now he begins to think that this was not good enough.

This is, no doubt, a sad story. A pleasant, decent man, in the prime of life, succumbs to a mysterious illness. His friends and colleagues cannot wait until he vacates his position in the government service. To his family his illness is a burden, and they are impatient for him to die. But why is this a story about alienation? Where is the life that is not understood or the society in which one feels oneself a stranger? Ivan Ilych knows what he is about; his life is as he wants it—pleasant and decorous. He fills his position competently and he knows it. He does not feel particularly powerless, nor does he deplore his lack of control over his circumstances. Everything seems to be going well; he has all the control he needs and what he does not understand does not disturb him. Not only does he not feel marginal among other men and women, but he is popular; he has a group of male companions with whom he regularly plays bridge and he is a good player and liked for that reason. There is in his life none of the uncertainty and confusion of the alienated, none of the aimless depression described earlier. He got the life he wanted until he fell ill. What more could any man want?

But Tolstoy sees it differently. Ivan Ilych's life is not merely unfortunate because he had the really bad luck of falling ill. As Tolstoy tells it, Ivan's life took a wrong turn very early on. He caroused with his fellow students and perhaps went to a prostitute.

> At school he had done things which had formerly seemed to him very horrid and made him feel disgusted with himself when he did them; but when later on he saw that these things were done by people of good position and that they did not regard them as wrong, he was able not exactly to regard them as right, but to forget about them entirely.... (p. 105)

While still a student, Ivan Ilych confronts the choice whether to take seriously his own conscience and his own feelings about what is right and what is wrong, or whether to go along with everyone else, so as not to stick out and be different. He chooses to conform. He therefore not only does things that he formerly had found disgusting but, worse, suppresses his doubts and unease about what he is doing. He simply turns away from his conscience and from moral issues, refusing to give them any thought. But in so doing he puts an end to all self-reflection, for he cannot continue to ignore his conscience and his own moral sense and at the same time reflect about his day-to-day actions or about the direction his life is taking. He also surrenders any critical stance toward the actions of others because he cannot assuage his self-doubt by saying "everybody does it" and then be critical of what everyone does. He cannot quiet some questions without silencing all of them. Once he silences his inner voice he must turn away from his inner life and live on the surface, without serious doubts, without indecision, without criticism of himself and others. Of necessity, he becomes a shallow, thoughtless person. In order to maintain his equanimity and not be plagued by doubts about his life, he needs to close off large parts of his person and stop thinking about how his life is going. The fault is not Ivan's alone. Tolstoy is at pains to castigate the shallowness of the entire society.

The consequences of this decision are grave. Cut off from his own feelings and critical self-reflection about his life, Ivan becomes a thorough conformist, instead of leading a life of his own. When his wife fell in love with him and everyone around him seemed to approve of the match, he said to himself "Why not?" and married her. He loved his wife in a way, but he made his decision without serious reflection. We can be sure that the engaged couple talked about the house they wanted and whom they would invite to their parties. The preparations for their wedding, we can be sure, were deeply concerned about clothes, the bride's trousseau, and the furnishing for their new house. They probably did not involve conversations about marriage and the life they were entering into, about difficulties they might encounter and how they would together face them.

For the first year they were happy because they were having fun together. But her pregnancy made Ivan Ilych's wife tense and irritable. Unable to leave the house, she begins to worry that she is less attractive to him and makes jealous scenes when he goes out. He, instead of trying to comfort her, stays out late playing bridge with his cronies because marriage is no longer fun. There is no deep connection between them; marriage is not about sharing one's life but about having fun. Thus Ivan cuts himself off from giving and receiving love; his wife becomes bitter and angry. They fight a lot and by the time Ivan Ilych falls ill, she has ceased to care what happens to him. She and his daughter are angry at him for being ill and repeat that it is his own fault for not following the doctors' instructions and taking his medicine.

Ivan Ilych assumes that life could always be comfortable and pleasant. As Tolstoy tells it, he only once confronts the question of what was right to do, he only once encounters the deep uncertainties that a life lived thoughtfully faces constantly. The choice of work, or of marriage partner, leaves many persons deeply disturbed because it is impossible to know at the moment of decision whether one is making the right choice. But Ivan's life choices come about thoughtlessly because uncertainty has no place in his world. His work does not raise troublesome questions for him. His entire life is designed to evade the reality felt so acutely by the alienated: that life is very uncertain, that often you cannot know what you should do, that it is difficult to understand who you are. Ivan has avoided true friendship and deep love because they are too difficult, too fraught with disappointment and loss. For him, relations to other persons, too, needed always to be pleasant and therefore remained entirely on the surface. Evading pain and doubt was the main work he has chosen for himself.

But in the end, for all his evasions, Ivan Ilych must face up to the fact that life is fundamentally uncertain because we all die and do not know when or under what conditions. Neither do we know what other disasters will befall us. Ivan Ilych is alienated even though he denies the reality of human life: that we find ourselves in a place we did not choose, as persons we did not decide to be, confronting tasks imposed by sheer accident. We try to make some sense of this opaque life that is given to us and try to direct it onto a good path under circumstances as unexpected as they are often contrary to our most fervent wishes. Ivan's life is single-mindedly devoted to concealing from himself that human lives are not ever transparent, but it is not for all that any less alienated. A society that encourages a life like Ivan's alienates—that is Tolstoy's message. In the chapters that follow, I will explain this in much more detail.

Only once does Ivan Ilych try to be his own person. When moving to a different city, he sets about furnishing the house he bought. He becomes totally engrossed in his task, choosing all appointments with the greatest care. He wants his house just his way—his one effort to have something distinctively his own to express his unique personality. But he fails. "His house was so like others, that it would never have been noticed"(p. 116). For the sake of living pleasantly, he has for many years avoided conflict. He has refused to be different, to go his own way because that would have been trouble. Always going along with what he thinks is expected of him, with what the "better sort of people" think and do, has left Ivan Ilych a shallow person without any ideas of his own. He has never learned to examine his life independently and to make independent choices. We are not born with this independence; we acquire it very slowly and with effort over a lifetime. Ivan Ilych, having resigned himself to living up to the expectations of the "better people," has never developed the requisite skills for doing anything on his own. His sudden desire to sever himself from everybody else's ideas and tastes ends predictably in embarrassment.

Gregor Samsa's life was so without meaning that his metamorphosis into a giant cockroach is not really surprising to anyone. It is just one more absurdity in a life that makes no sense whatsoever, where even the most mundane events are as senseless as his transformation. But persons whose life makes no sense and serves no purpose are not important, their actions do not matter, they have no contribution to make to the life of others. Being persons of little or no worth, they cannot have self-respect. Why should they not find themselves transformed into a cockroach? After all, they had suspected themselves of being disgusting insects all along. Empty lives deprive us of self-esteem. Ivan Ilych's modest wealth, his social position, and his power protect his sense of himself against the ravages of a life that is not really his own but is lived for him by others. What saves him for a while is his power over other people. One can, and many do, conceal their powerlessness in their own lives by controlling the lives of others. Dominating others, whether they be the physician's patients, the teacher's students, or subordinates at work, helps distract attention from one's own life, from the unknown forces that govern and the unforeseen events that disrupt it. The power one yields over others in business, in law, in the military, mimics power over one's own life but, because it diverts attention from the opacity and accidental nature of that life, it actually deepens alienation. As long as he is well, Ivan Ilych appears to have no problems of self-esteem because he can distract himself with the respect of his subordinates in the office and the flattery of the accused persons who come before him.

The hero of Fyodor Dostoyevsky's *Notes from the Underground* is not so fortunate. As a retired government clerk he has no money, no position, no work, and no power. His relative deprivations, however, leave him without illusions about the emptiness of his life and he understands how that emptiness corrodes his person:

> Why, we do not even know where to find real life, or what it is, or what it is called. . . . [W]e shall not know what to cling to, what to hold on to, what to love and what to hate, what to respect and what to despise. We even find it hard to be men, men of real flesh and blood, our own flesh and blood" (Dostoyevsky n.d.:240).

Without power or a prominent social position to conceal that they have no control over their lives, the alienated are terribly insecure. Overwhelmed by the sheer contingency of their existence, by events that are often as unexpected as they are disturbing, the alienated have no sense of their identity or the direction of their lives. But aimless, formless lives, having little value, do not inspire pride. Left without self-esteem the alienated are everywhere looking for affirmation, struggling for attention and for recognition from others. Their entire person seems a mere facade, a brave front to hide the complete absence of what one might call a "self."[1] Most persons seek their self-identity in the views others have of them; their identity does not flow from their own choices about what matters in work, ways of life, companions. Ivan Ilych's self-esteem depends on others' good opinion, but since he is fortunately placed in society, it is not so obvious that his sense of self-worth is quite precarious. But there can be no doubt about the deep insecurities of the young men in *Notes from the Underground*. They constantly seek the company and recognition of others more self-assured and well-to-do than they. If brash and self-confident Zverkov, owner of a small estate sporting the splendid uniform of an army officer, is willing to dine with them and seems to like them, then they too can like themselves and be self-assured. But such dependent selves are very fragile. Zverkov may get tired of them and find fancier friends; he is, in fact, going away. Then their self-esteem crumbles again. The man who tells us his sorry story in *Notes* is accordingly emotionally unstable; he takes "offense without rhyme or reason"; he is sensing slights everywhere. Selves not their own need permanent support by other persons; they are in constant danger of rejection, or disregard. Such a life is difficult because one is always on the brink of violent anger over slights, real or imagined, that destroy one's fragile self-esteem.

Friendships among persons with such ill-defined selves are troubled by distrust, by fear of rejection, by fear of being ridiculed. Constant jockeying for recognition disturbs every contact. One has friends not to share good times, or to give and receive affection, but only to get the recognition one needs to preserve equanimity. One does not give to anyone because one is always looking to receive. At best, one flatters the other so that one will be flattered in return. Real friendships deepen as one shares the other's life, but there is little to share in lives mainly ruled by accident or convention. Intimacy deepens friendship, but intimacy requires mutual trust. One wants to know that one's secrets are safe, that one will not be judged, that one will not be laughed at, or patronized. But if selves are too precarious, trust is impossible. One's self-confidence must be sufficiently sturdy to face possible misunderstandings or betrayal. The alienated lack that confidence; intimacy is therefore impossible for them. Their friendships are deliberately casual and insignificant like those of Ivan Ilych.

Like Ivan himself, the narrator in *Notes* can feel affection and love but cannot sustain a loving relationship. To do so requires that he make himself vulnerable to the other, that he give without expecting a return, that he accept gifts without fear that a price will be exacted for accepting them, that he share control with the person loved. The narrator in *Notes* feels love, but the need to maintain his self-esteem quickly gains the upper hand and he transforms love into a power struggle. As soon as he encounters love, he is frightened by the risk of rejection and rebuilds his defenses. After showing genuine kindness to Lisa, he begins to dominate her and destroys the openness and equality of love. Love means surrendering some control to the other person; but since he has no control in his own life, he needs to control other persons, much as Ivan Ilych does in his job, and therefore he cannot sustain love.

Freedom

"The only freedom which deserves the name is that of pursuing our own good in our own way, so long as we do not attempt to deprive others of theirs" (Mill 1948:11).

In this brief sentence John Stuart Mill summarizes a very common understanding of freedom. Free men and women must not be prevented by government or by social pressures from pursuing, in the way they think best, the ends they have chosen for themselves. To be free one must be able to live one's own life as one sees fit and leave others the same liberty. But what shall we say about Ivan Ilych, who does not pursue his own good in his own way? His freedom is curtailed neither by government nor oppressive neighbors but by his own unwillingness to brave the uncertainties and confusions of a life not governed by the ideas of others. To the extent that Ivan Ilych seems to surrender his freedom to conventions, we might be tempted to say that he is free but has opted not to exercise that freedom. (But does not Ivan Ilych, in bowing to convention, choose his own good? The answer to that question will have to wait until Chapter 5.) He could, if he wanted to, pursue his own good in his own way but prefers to pursue a good that others prescribe for him. Restraints on the exercise of one's freedom chosen by a person herself leaves her as free as before. Only constraints externally imposed abridge freedom. (There are, of course, external restraints other than government or private repression. Freedom is constrained by poverty, by discrimination, by ill health.)

This conception of freedom assumes that unless persons are prevented from living life as they please by forces external to them, they are free. But are there not also internal forces that prevent us from pursuing the good as we see it? Consider persons who are clear about what they want but whose pursuits are thwarted by an addiction to gambling. Others are prevented from pursuing their own good by excessive timidity, because they are too frightened by the risks involved in pursuing the good as they see it in their more courageous moments. Or think of Ivan Ilych, finally, in furnishing his new house, trying to strike out on his own by putting his personal stamp on the house but failing miserably because he has never learned to be independent and to think and choose for himself. We are not born knowing how to live our own lives, but have to learn that. If we fail to acquire the necessary independence of mind, are we still free? It would seem that freedom can also be thwarted by impediments internal to the person and that this is as harsh a constraint on our freedom as the government's threat of imprisonment or death, or our neighbors' threat of social ostracism.

Thus freedom belongs only to those who, being fortunate enough to be allowed to run their own lives within certain limits, actually are able to do so. In that sense, Ivan Ilych is not free, nor is the interlocutor of *Notes from the Underground*. The inner life of the narrator in *Notes* is so chaotic that he has no attention left to ask what would be a good life for him. The constant agitation of trying to get any recognition at all from anyone makes it impossible for him to think about his good or to set out to reach it. He says: "[W]e shall not know what to cling to, what to hold on to, what to love and what to hate, what to respect and what to despise." He cannot pursue his own good in his own way because he cannot even think clearly what his own good might be. Ivan Ilych is too frightened of the uncertainties besetting the search for his own good to have any opinions of his own; not for him are the confusions of those who recognize that it may be difficult to say what their good is, who know that it may prove impossible to reach because human life is full of uncertainty and sudden disaster. Mill's freedom is as inaccessible to the alienated as it is to the prisoner in solitary confinement.

Formless existence and lack of identity prevent the alienated from shaping their own lives. Devoid of self-esteem, they are dependent on the approbation of others, and that imposes strict limitations on how they live. To that extent their freedom is limited. Alienation limits freedom as effectively as open coercion.

Some Serious Reservations

My examples raise the question of whether alienation afflicts everyone's life. I told the story of the narrator from *Notes from the Underground* as a typical example of one kind of alienation, but when I consider the narrator in Dostoyevsky's story, I do not recognize myself. Yes, everyone occasionally feels insecure and needs the approval of others, but no one I know spends all his time or all her energy getting attention from others. Not even very small children, who thrive on being noticed, are exclusively preoccupied with getting attention. Nor are most persons as cavalier in making choices as Ivan Ilych. The choice of work, or of marriage partner, is usually carefully considered. Unlike Ivan Ilych and his wife, we do not think of pregnancy or serious illness among family or friends as mere inconveniences. No doubt, some of us lead more exciting lives than others, but the mindless monotony of Gregor Samsa's life does not represent common experience.

We need to ask ourselves whether these stories succeed in holding up a mirror to us or whether they are, at best, overdrawn caricatures of ordinary lives. Their authors, Kafka, Tolstoy, and Dostoyevsky, expect us to see ourselves reflected in their heroes, but it is not self-evident that we must take these portrayals quite so seriously. More explanations of alienation will be required to convince us that it is a central problem in our lives.

We must also admit that the account given so far has not established even that such a condition as alienation exists.

For one thing, to many readers of *Notes* the narrator may well appear as a pathological figure. The story is powerful, but should we perhaps describe its main character as "very peculiar" or "bizarre" rather than as "alienated"? We might think that not much is to be learned here about the lives of ordinary people. Ivan Ilych is an unfortunate man. He is not a bad sort. He grows up in a certain family and social milieu, and he does pretty much what everybody else does. Human beings are, after all, social animals. We learn how to live by imitating those around us. It seems carping to call that "conformism" and to be critical of it. How else is one supposed to learn how to live? Ivan's marriage is, on the whole, a failure, and he may bear some responsibility for that. But falling ill is clearly a misfortune and he suffers accordingly. We should pity him perhaps, or his social situation, but not decry his life as alienated.

In addition, we need to ask whether the concept of alienation adds anything to the discussion of suffering in human lives. Yes, people are sometimes depressed, they distrust themselves, they lack confidence in their abilities and do not trust others to love and support them. People are, sometimes, bored or at loose ends. All of this is familiar. What is gained by gathering up these different experiences of depression, distrust of self and others, and boredom under the concept of "alienation"?

As we begin this extended reflection about the concept of alienation we must be aware that the concept itself is controversial.[2] What may appear to some people to be ordinary misfortune, or some sort of pathology, is by others interpreted as alienation. It is tempting to think of the narrator in *Notes from the Underground* as neurotic rather than as alienated. Ivan Ilych, we might say, is not alienated but, instead, cannot enjoy life because he is ill. Implicit in these different characterizations of the two literary figures are different *explanations* of unhappiness. Most common is the idea that depression or aimlessness is to be cured by going out, having fun, diverting oneself, going shopping, traveling, moving to a new house, perhaps changing one's job or life partner. Alternative explanations of depression and boredom seek the causes in childhood experiences to be remembered and overcome in one kind of psychotherapy or another.

In our world, many people believe that going out and having fun are all that the depressed, the lonely, the distrustful need. Many people also subscribe to one psychotherapeutic methodology or another. Few consider explicitly the questions about the meaning of their life: Do they control it in any way, and does it form a coherent whole or not? Speaking of alienation becomes necessary because not all unhappiness can be cured by having more fun or doing psychotherapy. Unhappiness, depression, lack of purpose in one's life are *also* due to alienation, in ways that will be explained in great detail in the chapters that follow.

The theory of alienation implies that what matters in human life is whether it makes sense, whether it is unified in some way. In discussions of alienation, people who are "themselves" or are "their own person" are contrasted with others whose lives are given over to convention, to pleasing everyone else at the expense of their independence. A definite conception of the good life for human beings underlies these discussions of alienation—one that is quite different from the more common conceptions, especially those repeated endlessly by mass media and advertisers, of the good life as the pursuit of anything that promises pleasure for the moment. We need to examine, in the chapters that follow, what that conception is before we can decide that alienation exists and is a threat to human freedom.

Notes

1. We shall see in Chapter 3 that this talk about a "self" is confusing because it suggests a more solid core of personal identity than we in fact possess.

2. Occasionally even newspapers participate in polemics against the concept of alienation. On July 2, 2001, various newspapers ran a column in which George Will used the fiftieth anniversary of the first publication of J. D. Salinger's *The Catcher in the Rye* to ridicule talk about alienation as an affectation of academic intellectuals (*Worcester Telegram and Gazette*, July 2, 2001, p. A6).

2

The History of the
Concept of Alienation

We begin this chapter fully aware that the concept of alienation is controversial. The stories we examined in the previous chapter and read as portrayals of alienation may also be understood as the story of an unfortunate civil servant—Ivan Ilych—and of another one who is quite mad—the narrator in *Notes from the Underground*. But, as we shall see, several outstanding philosophers have paid serious attention to the notion of alienation. Not only did they regard it as a real condition, but they expended considerable energy in order to clarify it. These important thinkers did indeed believe that alienation exists in our world, and they characterized it for us in ways that we cannot help but accept as part of human reality. They also provide us with some excellent arguments against those who reject alienation as idle fancy. At the end of this chapter we will have more reasons for taking alienation seriously.

This will be a fragmentary history, but one that deepens our understanding of the nature of alienation by presenting the thought of four philosophers who reflected quite deeply about this subject. In the course of these historical studies we will see how, throughout the eighteenth and nineteenth centuries, the concept of alienation became much more complex than before. We will also see how, in some respects, these different accounts are incomplete, one-sided, or misleading. Marx, Kierkegaard, and Nietzsche had read Rousseau, but they were not influences on each other's writings. Marx and Kierkegaard, though contemporaries, did not know of each other's work. And Nietzsche, who came later, read Kierkegaard late in his life after he had done his important thinking about alienation. But the four of them lived through different portions of the Enlightenment and its nineteenth century aftermath, and the changes occurring in the world at large during that entire period are reflected in the progressively more complex conceptions of alienation found in their works.

Rousseau

Jean-Jacques Rousseau was born in 1712, in the Swiss republic of Geneva. Rousseau's mother died in childbirth; his father had to flee Geneva after a quarrel and left the young Jean-Jacques in the care of relatives. At the age of sixteen, Rousseau ran away from Geneva and drifted from place to place for the next fourteen years. In 1742, now thirty, he arrived in Paris, eager to make a name for himself as a musician. He struck up friendships with some of the great Enlightenment writers, such as Diderot, Voltaire, and D'Alembert. But he was only moderately successful and never felt at ease in Paris. He distrusted the very civilized ways of Parisian society and was often critical of just those institutions that inspired the greatest pride in most others, his friends included. He died in 1778, alone and scorned by many who, in earlier years, had admired him and sought his company.

Quite characteristically his first published work, *Discourse on the Sciences and the Arts* (1750), argues that the progress made in the arts and sciences, which had brought back Europe from the darkness of medieval times, had not really improved the lot of humankind. Contrary to what most of his contemporaries believed, Rousseau thought that this progress had produced moral decay, cowardice, and lack of freedom.

> Today . . . a vile and deceiving uniformity reigns in our midst, and all minds seem to have been cast in the same mold: constant politeness demands, propriety commands; constantly one follows custom, never one's own genius. One no longer dares to appear what one is. . . . One will thus never really know with whom one is dealing. . . . [There exist] no more sincere friendships. (Rousseau 1986:6)

Rousseau contrasts this state of civilized society with the state of nature. Such stories about natural man, or about human beings in the state of nature, were commonplace in the seventeenth and eighteenth centuries, and we can actually find them already in Plato's *Republic* two thousand years earlier. But whereas some writers (e.g., John Locke in England) thought that human beings in a "natural state" actually existed, Rousseau believed without doubt that the state of nature "no longer exists, perhaps never did exist, and probably never will exist; . . . it is nevertheless necessary to have true ideas [of it], in order to form a true judgment of our present state" (Rousseau 1950:190–191).

In other words, the state of nature is a useful fiction for the purposes of understanding our current condition. Late in his life, Rousseau explained that this story about the state of nature showed us that

> nature made man happy and good, but that society depraves him and
> makes him miserable. . . . [The story] makes us see the human race
> as better, wiser, and happier in its primitive constitution; blind, mis-
> erable and wicked to the degree that it moves away from it . . . but
> human nature does not move backwards. (Rousseau 1990:213)

At one time, Rousseau thought, natural man lived essentially by himself,
or in families. In this natural state, human beings were free, they were
good, they were happy. Human beings come into the world "happy and
good"; it is society that corrupts them and renders them "miserable and
wicked." He is eloquent in the moral condemnation of his contemporaries and of himself.

> That is how luxury, dissoluteness, and slavery have at all times been
> the punishment visited upon our prideful efforts to leave the happy
> ignorance in which eternal wisdom has placed us. . . . What will be-
> come of virtue when one has to become rich at all costs? The an-
> cient political thinkers forever spoke of morals and virtue; ours speak
> only of commerce and money. (Rousseau 1986:13, 16)

This passage primarily expresses Rousseau's moral disapproval of his contemporaries. They are beset by "dissoluteness" and lack of "virtue." But
alienation and immorality are distinct, even though Rousseau is not always
quite clear about that. Clearly, the alienated can be as immoral as the mul-
titudes whose lead they follow. Yet if public opinion and standards of behavior are saintly, so are the alienated who surrender their self-identities to
the dictates of this saintly public. Conversely, it is possible to be one's own
person but to be evil nevertheless.

But Rousseau also draws attention to alienation explicitly when he
writes that in society one "constantly . . . follows custom, never one's own
genius. One no longer dares to appear what one is" (Rousseau 1990:6).
Each tries to appear to be acceptable to all the others by following "custom"—the prevailing conventions—rather than their own inclinations,
beliefs, and values. None dare show themselves as they are; they are not
themselves. Here Rousseau diagnoses the ills in society in the same terms
that Tolstoy uses to portray the life of Ivan Ilych. Alienation is rampant because people, instead of trying to be themselves, succumb to the demands
of society and arrange their lives to meet fashion's demands. The goal for
all of us, Rousseau thinks, is to be ourselves: "To be something, to be himself, and always at one with himself, a man must act as he speaks, must
know what course he ought to take, and must follow that course with

vigor and persistence" (Rousseau 1993:8). We should teach each child to
". . . live rather than to avoid death; life is not breath but action, the use of
our senses, our mind, our faculties, every part of ourselves that makes us
conscious of our being. Life consists less in length of days than in the keen
sense of living" (Rousseau 1993:11). We are not ourselves, not "at one"
with ourselves, because we lack a sense of what life is about. This would
require that we have plans for our life—that we "know what course . . . to
take" in terms of career, when to marry, how many children to have, and
when to retire. We must have a clear sense of what is a good life. We
should be clear about what we consider good and evil, important and trivial. We should not have to reflect at great length or hesitate before we decide that we will not lie or cheat, take advantage of the weakness of others,
or get ahead at all costs. Nor should we have to depend on others for our
sense of how to live, of what is important and what is not.

Having a plan, a picture of the good life, is, however, not enough; neither
is a clear sense of what one regards as valuable. One must follow one's plan
"with vigor and persistence"; one must make an active and sustained effort
to live well and make good use of one's time. Goals are real for us only if we
actually pursue them; only those values are real for me that animate my actions. One must "act as [s/]he speaks." Just saying that one has these values is
not sufficient. Hypocrisy or flagrant self-deception may well be symptoms of
alienation. Firmly in possession of oneself, one does not hide one's values but
puts them forward unambiguously for all to see. Where necessary, one stands
up for one's values and defends them because those who attack them attack
one's self. Timidity in the assertion of one's values betokens a wavering identity. Excessive eagerness to fight on behalf of one's values, on the other hand,
may be a symptom of the same unease with oneself.

But one must form one's ideas about one's life in accord with what is possible. To the extent that there is always a discrepancy between desire and
power, one is alienated. "True happiness consists in decreasing the difference
between our desires and our powers, in establishing a perfect equilibrium
between the power and the will" (Rousseau 1993:52). Some might understand this as a counsel of resignation, that one should not want other than
what one has. Instead, Rousseau is warning us not to misunderstand this picture of being oneself. It would be a mistake to think of self-possessed persons, following their plans and values, as constantly striving, of being forever
dissatisfied with what they have because it falls short of their life goals, of
looking forever toward the future and not savoring the delights of the present. Making one's life one's own is not that. "Life consists less in length of
days than in the keen sense of living." Persons who have made their lives
their own live energetically with a "keen sense of living" in the present.

Alienation displays itself in listlessness, boredom, and disinterest in the world around us. But it also displays itself in frantic activity, in constant striving, in looking toward an imagined, hoped-for future, devaluing thereby what one has already accomplished and the life one leads. Those who are forever striving for new and higher goals always fall short; they are never adequate to the tasks they have set themselves. Failure is unavoidable because whatever they attain is never enough; it is always inferior to a more resplendent future. As a consequence, "Civilized man . . . is always moving, sweating and toiling. . . . " Forever dissatisfied, the alienated human being is always striving for more, striving to be better, and pursuing a success that is always deferred. Therefore, "[he] lives constantly outside himself, and only knows how to live in the opinions of others, so that he seems to receive the consciousness of his own existence merely from the judgment of others concerning him" (Rousseau 1993:270). Striving ceaselessly, one always falls short. Constant failure, then, affects one's trust in one's own wisdom; the goals one sets for oneself, which seem so unattainable, become discredited and one substitutes commonly followed goals for one's own aims and judgments of the broad public for one's own opinions. One's sense of oneself comes to depend on the opinions of others. Subjected to public opinion and the demands of prevailing ideas, one loses one's independence. "Our wisdom is slavish prejudice, our customs consist in control, constraint, compulsion. Civilized man is born and dies a slave . . . All life long, man is imprisoned by our institutions. . . . " (Rousseau 1993:11)

Not content with the life they lead, alienated persons seek approval from others because they cannot provide it for themselves. Having set themselves goals they are unable to meet, they seek to assuage their sense of failure by getting approval from others. They look to others for approbation and will do whatever those others expect of them in order to get their approval. They are no longer pleasing themselves but seek only to please others, and their life is no longer their own. They lose their autonomy and with it their freedom. They become, in Rousseau's language, "slaves," servile, deferential to the powerful, flattering anyone who can further their career and help them attain the fame they seek. Pleasing anonymous others takes the place of being pleased about themselves and their life. Sales figures for books replace one's considered judgment about one's own work; one likes the songs one sings as long as they are played on the radio; the goal of being the most popular teacher shapes one's demeanor in the classroom. I consider myself attractive because my clothes are the work of a famous designer. I like my house because it has a "good address."

If you lead your own life, and your plans are within your power, you can take pleasure in your accomplishments. Rousseau calls that "self-love" and distinguishes it from "pride." Self-love comes from being strong, living one's life one's own way, and being content with what one has and does. Pride is for those who lack self-love and instead primarily seek affirmation in the eyes of others. One takes pride in what others admire, in the acclaim one earns for pleasing society. But being proud, one lacks self-love, and is thus alienated. "When man is content to be himself he is strong indeed; when he strives to be more than man he is weak indeed" (Rousseau 1993:53). A life lived as one chooses according to what one considers important is a life affirmed and enjoyed. Persons who live such a life are content. They are strong because they are equal to the demands their life makes on them. They are competent in the world that is theirs; they can do what they need to do.

Rousseau's stories about natural man, who lived by himself quite happily being fully himself, allow him to show that alienation is not an inescapable part of human life. We can well imagine, Rousseau tells us, human beings who are like us in some ways but different in others, because their circumstances are very different from ours. The problems we have in being ourselves, in fully owning ourselves, are unknown in the state of nature. Alienation is a problem that arises in some social settings; if we can change those social settings, it can perhaps be overcome. But since alienation is a social ill connected to a particular society, one cannot escape it by making individual choices. I cannot, by myself, reconstruct my life so as to lessen alienation. It can be eased only through a transformation of the society in which we live; there are no private escapes for the lucky few enlightened enough to be able to start anew. Rousseau did not believe that we need to return to the mythical state of nature to be ourselves. Obviously such a return is not possible; equally obviously it would be totally undesirable. But we *can* alter the fundamental features of our society in order to alleviate alienation.

Rousseau's is the first lengthy discussion of alienation in the history of Western philosophy. His central insight—that there are varying degrees of being a person in one's own right, of having a clear self of one's own, and that some people are themselves and others are not—is right on target. But when we ask Rousseau what it means to be a person in one's own right, his answer is not quite adequate, as we shall see in the chapters that follow. Rousseau is right in thinking that a person who lives her own life is likely to live it more energetically than someone who is adrift and dependent on others for direction. He is also right in believing that alienation weakens self-esteem. But lacking a self, lacking a clear identity, is not best identified as conformism.

The conception of alienation as subjection to others, to public opinion and convention, invites the same questions that arose at the end of the last chapter in connection with the story of Ivan Ilych. Humans are born helpless. At birth we are not fully developed persons and have to learn slowly and painfully over many years how to be full human beings. We learn this not independently, on our own, but from parents, siblings, peers, and the society at large. We learn from others how to think and what to think, and we think with and against others who consider similar questions about the good life. Our self-esteem is inevitably shaped by the opinions of others. Pride in my work depends on competence assessed by others. It would be strange to be proud of work that no one considered competent. Human lives are lived with others; we owe a great deal to those others and are dependent on them for our understanding of the world and of ourselves. Being oneself cannot mean complete independence from all others. Only wolf children—children who grow up in the wild outside of human society—are completely independent from human society. But they also have no human speech or knowledge of how humans act. As humans we depend on our human group for initiating us into our humanity and helping us maintain it. (See the sections titled "Self-Esteem" and "Recognition" in Chapter 3.)

Alienation is not best understood as arising from the struggle with others whose ideas, values, and demands dominate our lives. The problems and conditions in which alienation overcomes us are much more complex than that. But Rousseau was right in stressing that alienation arises more readily in some social settings than in others. In order to lessen alienation, to make a life of one's own, to get some modicum of control over one's life, and give it a sense of some kind, one needs to learn how to be oneself, how to give some sort of shape to one's life, and how to give it meaning. But those skills are not easily learned, and we are fortunate when life forces us to learn them. In some societies, it is easier to learn them. In others, learning to lead one's own life is fraught with difficulties (see Chapter 4). Rousseau's view of alienation as enslavement by society suggests that the alienated have made a bad choice, and if they could only be prevailed upon to make a different choice, alienation could be overcome. But as we shall see, as our story unfolds, the role of personal choice in overcoming alienation is complex. It is at least as much a matter of luck, fortunate accident, and surrounding social conditions as a matter of our own choices if we learn how to live differently, more on our own as well as more fully with others.

Kierkegaard

Søren Kierkegaard was born in 1813 in Copenhagen, Denmark, to a wealthy merchant, the youngest of seven children. His father was both deeply religious

and depressive, as were Søren and his older brother Peter. Peter became a
bishop in the Danish Lutheran Church; Søren, its fiercest critic. In his writings he attacked Lutheranism—the state religion—and incurred the enmity
of most "right thinking" citizens of Copenhagen. Except for one extended
stay in Berlin and two shorter trips there, he never left Denmark and even
rarely left Copenhagen. An engagement broken by him a few months before
the wedding caused him great agony, which reverberated in many of his writings. During the last ten years of his life, Kierkegaard poured out an astonish-
ing array of different writings, ranging from difficult philosophical texts to
lyrical sermons. He collapsed in the street in 1855, while handing out leaflets
critical of the Lutheran Church, and died a month later.

Since he spent a lifetime attacking the established church, it may seem
surprising that Kierkegaard described himself as a religious author
(Kierkegaard 1962:5–6). But religion did not mean to him what it meant
to the pastors and faithful of the Danish Lutheran Church: a theology, specific rituals, the church as an organization. What mattered above all to
Kierkegaard was the religious life of the individual. The important question was not whether God exists, or whether the teachings of this or that
church are true. Now that may seem strange, for if God did not exist, how
could one lead a religious life? But Kierkegaard replied to that with a
question of his own: Would God's existence be of any importance whatsoever if it did not make a difference in human lives? God's existence does
not guarantee us a religious life, one in which God's existence is the central reality. The challenge for the individual person is not to find proofs for
the existence of God, nor to do what the priest tells us to do; rather, it is
"to become a Christian"—that is, to live in such a way that God's presence
permeates everyday life. To be a religious person, particularly a Christian, is
a matter of living life in a particular way. Only rarely are human beings
born with the ability to lead that sort of life; they must learn to do that.
Hence the question is how to become a Christian—that is, how to learn
to live a life in which the Christian God is the central reality.

Ordinarily, human beings are "in despair." That phrase meant for
Kierkegaard what it means for us: to be unhappy or depressed, to find no
meaning or purpose in life. But, more than that, it refers to an underlying
condition of human beings that these emotions manifest. In describing this
fundamental condition Kierkegaard used the same terms that Rousseau
used to describe alienation. Despair is the condition of the person who
"does not possess himself, he is not himself" (Kierkegaard 1941b:27). "Despair" was Kierkegaard's name for alienation.

Kierkegaard's main example of alienation was what he called the "aesthetic life," in which the goal is to have pleasure—much as Ivan Ilych

sought to live pleasantly and decorously. Moral philosophers, such as hedonists or utilitarians, have often argued that pleasure is the only "unqualified good," as John Stuart Mill (1949) put it. Kierkegaard disagreed with that, but not for the reasons usually adduced in philosophical debates. There the widespread opinion is that devoting oneself to a life of pleasure is morally reprehensible. A morally good person, many philosophers assert, does what is right, even if doing what is right is not always pleasant. The hedonist is incapable of doing that if he is consistent; hence hedonism is immoral. Kierkegaard, by contrast, believed that the single-minded pursuit of pleasure alienates. The trouble with a life devoted to the pursuit of pleasure is not primarily that it is immoral—although Kierkegaard believed that, too—but that it leaves one without a clear self-identity.

Like Tolstoy, Kierkegaard thought that the pleasure-seeking life is motivated by avoidance of the more serious task of giving meaning to one's life, having an identity of one's own, and shaping one's life to one's own purposes. But unlike Rousseau and Tolstoy, Kierkegaard did not really condemn the pursuit of pleasure; instead, he emphasized the futility and suffering of a hedonist project because a life dedicated to the pursuit of pleasure is self-defeating. Pleasures do not bear repetition well. What pleases the first few times soon becomes stale; then new and different pleasures are needed. A pleasure-seeking life is always threatened by boredom, which deprives life of meaning. Without novelty to sharpen the appetites, pleasure seeking soon degenerates into a repetitive round of the same, now stale, entertainments. A repetitive life has no more sense than a tune that repeats the same few notes over and over, or the story that keeps returning to its beginning to retell the same events. Such a life is burdensome because it is empty; we need to fill up our time, or even "kill" it. There is, moreover, no continuity in a life of pleasure. One rushes from one entertainment to another; anything that pleases is worth doing. But the different pleasures are not connected; there is no sustained story in such a life. It lacks any sense.

These ideas of Kierkegaard's require some explanation, for the reader may well object that many people lead pleasant lives doing the same work for many years, sharing their lives with the same person, living in the same house on the same street, and passing their days in the same round of activities. Kierkegaard would not have denied that these are "good" lives, but he also would not have said that they are lives of pleasure. He meant "pleasure" in the fairly literal sense of "fun"; the pursuit of pleasure is the pursuit of laughter, intense pleasure, strong sensations. In such lives, commitment, habit, life projects play no role because all of these involve long periods that we could not really call pleasurable. Persons pursuing the life of pleasure will act or not act because doing so is "fun" and for no other reason. They have no life plan, no long-term projects; whether their life has any coherence or makes sense is no concern of theirs.

For us to find pleasure, conditions must be right. A delicious meal is not enjoyed by the sick; under gray skies an otherwise pleasing landscape depresses. Accidental conditions, not under our control, determine whether we find pleasure or not (see the section titled "Faint Friendships, Tepid Love" in Chapter 4). Whether we reach our goal of finding pleasure is not up to us because fortuitous external conditions, which we do not control, decide that for us. In the pursuit of pleasure, we limit our autonomy because we place ourselves at the mercy of contingent events that decide whether pleasures will be ours or not (Kierkegaard 1959, vol. II:184).

Pleasures come and go; hardship is a part of every life. But the pleasure seekers are not prepared to face the inevitable sorrows. They lack the resources to meet the inevitable pains of life and to bear them bravely (Kierkegaard 1959, vol. II:81). In the never-ending search for diversion, persons do not firm up their character; they are not equipped to live courageously when danger threatens. But it is in times of trouble that the question of meaning arises most insistently. As long as life is pleasant, one does not ask whether it has meaning. But when pleasure ends, when, as happened to Ivan Ilych, sickness and death threaten, or when one is bored, or at loose ends, the question comes up whether all this tedium and pain is worth living for. Then the question whether life is meaningful forces itself upon us. The aesthetic man, the hedonist, has no answer to that question. Being interested only in pleasure, and having no life project but only loosely connected experiences, the hedonist has no answer to the question whether that life, as a whole, serves a purpose; whether it has a justification, or makes some sense because it coheres in some way. In Volume I of his *Either/Or*, first published in 1843, Kierkegaard presents a rich tapestry of the experiences of pleasure seekers and the profound despair—depression, boredom, and desperation—that is the essence of that life. *Either/Or* provides a detailed and differentiated critique of the life of the likes of Ivan Ilych.

Here Kierkegaard addresses explicitly one of the controversies regarding alienation mentioned at the end of the preceding chapter. Not everyone believes that alienation is a real problem in human lives and many think that "whining about alienation," as they call it, is the pastime of privileged academics. Such critics of the notion of alienation hold that what matters in human lives is that they be pleasant, filled with joy and accomplishment, and all this talk about having a life of one's own, about the meaning of one's life, and about alienation is just so much nonsense. What matters is to get what one wants—nothing more. Kierkegaard gives us some serious reasons for distrusting that view. The question about the meaning of one's life, especially when it is troubled, is not an invention of idle intellectuals. In light of Kierkegaard's reflections about the futility of pleasure seeking and Rousseau's vivid descriptions of the difference between persons with a clear identity and those who are adrift in their lives, the critics of the concept of alienation will have difficulties convincing us that alienation does not need to be taken seriously. (I will return to this issue at the end of the chapter.)

Much like Tolstoy and Rousseau, Kierkegaard connects alienation with the overweening importance of public opinion: The alienated are

> as it were . . . defrauded by "the others." By seeing the multitude of men about [them], by getting engaged in all sorts of worldly affairs, by becoming wise about how things go in this world, such a man forgets himself, forgets his name, does not dare believe in himself, finds it too venturesome a thing to be himself, far easier and safer to be like the others, to become an imitation, a cipher in the crowd. (Kierkegaard 1941a:51)

But whereas Rousseau thought that it was of the essence of alienation to be enslaved to the opinions of others and to their expectations of us, Kierkegaard saw clearly that the tyranny of public opinion and of fashion is only a *manifestation* of alienation, its *result*. Alienation enfeebles selves, making it difficult not to constantly look over one's shoulder to see what the others are doing, and difficult to disagree with prevailing wisdom or to brave the disapproval of neighbors or colleagues. Alienated lives tend to drift because they lack direction; joining the crowd gives them some semblance of justification because they now seem to participate in a common project. Conformism is only the result of alienation, not its nature. But what then is alienation?

Kierkegaard's answer is, at first, obscure: "Man is a synthesis of the infinite and the finite, of the temporal and the eternal, of freedom and necessity" (1941b:46). The self is the self-conscious attempt to construct some sort of unity out of these opposing elements. Being oneself, struggling against alienation, is thus always an attempt to reconcile aspects of human existence that are in conflict with each other. In the course of *Sickness unto Death*, Kierkegaard develops a fairly complex typology of different failures to bridge the opposite sides of human existence. Alienation takes many different forms because so many different oppositions tear life apart. Their effects vary widely, as do the ways in which different persons struggle to overcome or, more often, to evade these conflicts.

Kierkegaard characterizes the opposing aspects of human life in terms that are in keeping with his religious preoccupations. Human beings are suspended between the material world and the eternal; they are free but also subject to God's law; they live in time but their salvation is in eternity. But this formulation is much too abstract to do full justice to Kierkegaard's insight that alienation arises because human beings are never all of one piece. Less abstractly put, our lives are fractured because we are animals but we are also thinking beings, because we are embodied but we also have minds that can roam far from the here and now, because we find ourselves thinking, feeling, and acting in ways that we did not choose and that surprise us while, at the same time, we are critical of our own thoughts, feelings, and actions, and those of others.

Human beings do not want to be lived by their lives; they want to live them purposefully. They do not want to be spectators of their lives but want to be in the thick of them, acting, giving direction. They want to be not objects of their lives but subjects, not victims but fully in control of their lives. They want to shape their lives and give them a meaning. They want to glory in the knowledge that they live their life as well as they know how. But those same human beings are, in Heidegger's (1929) striking phrase, *geworfen* (thrown) into this life. We are born unable to do much more than react subtly to those around us who must take care of us, if we are to survive. As human beings, we are not born fully competent to live in the world as clearly defined persons. It takes many years of apprenticeship to persons older than ourselves before we can begin to direct our own lives. These caretakers, who teach us, largely shape how we think about the world and about ourselves. We do not choose these caretakers and therefore do not choose the fundamental influences that mould our lives. We are born into situations and bodies that leave indelible imprints on our lives in ways that we discover only very slowly. We inherit personality traits, abilities, and defects, opportunities and deprivations that largely make our lives what they are, and our capacity for altering any of those capacities and traits is very limited. What is worse, we do not fully understand our situation, and even our own person is not transparent to us. We discover only very slowly who we are, what we can do, and even to the very end of life we surprise ourselves by being able to withstand hardship that we thought would exceed our power of toleration, or by thinking or feeling in ways of which we did not believe ourselves capable.

Were we not thinking beings, we could just follow the lead of contingent events and not be any the worse for it. But we not only are who, what, and where we happen to be but we also think, formulate goals, set standards, and criticize. We have wishes and ideals; we dream. But this thinking, reflecting, and dreaming being lives by means of an animal body, subject to often unintelligible and certainly unpredictable forces. Human lives are disrupted by this opposition: Caught between our deliberative and accidental natures, we are threatened by alienation.

Hedonism, what Kierkegaard calls the aesthetic life, is one attempt to escape these conflicting demands on us. If pleasure is all that counts, one does not need one's life to make sense, to have an intelligible history and go somewhere. One does not need to have clear convictions to try to live up to and to defend, if necessary. One floats along on the stream of life, paddling to get to pleasant spots and to avoid the occasional rocks under the surface of the water. One allows contingency full reign. One makes a virtue out of alienation. Utilitarianism is the ideology of the alienated.

Kierkegaard's insight, that human life is inherently disturbed by acute tensions, is of enormous importance for an understanding of alienation, but his account of the underlying tensions in human life is very schematic. He also did not pay sufficient attention to the effect of society on our ability to make something of our life. In different societies it is easier or harder to learn to reconcile the conflicting forces that impinge on us. Marx's analysis complements that of Kierkegaard by drawing attention to the influence of social structures on alienation.

Marx

Among the thinkers discussed here, Karl Marx is the most closely associated with the concept of alienation, even though his conception of alienation is found primarily in unpublished notebooks, written when he was still a young man. There he discusses alienation in a restricted context—namely, as it manifests itself in the lives of wage workers. The wage workers Marx had in mind differed from today's salaried professionals in that they had few skills. They just worked, not for the sake of work satisfaction, or in order to use and expand their skills, but merely for the money: They worked pretty much where they earned the most, selling their time and energy to the highest bidder without taking into account the character of the work they might have been required to do. The money earned was more important than the actual work. That worker, Marx wrote, "does not fulfill himself in his work but denies himself, has a feeling of misery rather than of well-being, does not develop freely his mental and physical energies. . . . [H]e does not belong to himself . . . " (Marx 1963:125). The wage workers are not their own persons; they cannot make anything of their lives or of themselves; they never get to be the persons they might have become under different circumstances because they lack the opportunities (free time, choice of work, education, chance to travel, etc.) to develop their capacities to make something meaningful of their lives.

Kierkegaard stressed that alienation originates in the tension in human lives between purposiveness and determination by accidents, whereas Marx reminded us that the burden of external forces, of the contingent and accidental, bears down more heavily on some groups than on others. One's position in the society determines the balance between autonomy and subjection to external conditions in one's life. Wage workers have considerably less scope for being persons in their own right. They are not their own boss. Whether they work, what they do, how much they get paid, and under what conditions they work are all decided by the owners of the factory, office, store, or school where they work.

In a society characterized by private property in the means of production, power is distributed very unevenly because the owners of workplaces have a great deal of power over the lives of people who need to work in order to live and to support their families. The wage workers tend to be dependent on their employers to a degree that the employers are not dependent on individual wage earners. Most wage workers are easily replaced; most employers are not.

Under conditions of private property, the workers receive wages, but what they produce belongs to the employer. At the end of the day they have some money to show for their work, but nothing else. There is no product they can take pride in, show off to their children and grandchildren, or put their mark on.

> It's not just the work. Somebody built the pyramids. Somebody's gonna build something. . . . I would like to see a building, say, the Empire State, I would like to see on one side of it a foot-wide strip from top to bottom with the name of every bricklayer, the name of every electrician, with all the names. So when a guy walked by, he could take his son and say, "See, that's me over there on the 45th floor. I put the steel beam in." Picasso can point to a painting. What can I point to? (Terkel 1974)

Not being independent craftsmen, workers do not organize their work; their product bears not their names but the name of their employer.

Work that one can take pride in, because it allows one to develop one's skills, augments self-esteem and strengthens one to resist threats and maintain equanimity in the face of the unexpected. So also is one's ability enhanced to shape one's life when work requires skills developed over many years and when one directs one's work and, in so doing, learns to direct one's life. But, Marx points out, much of the work done in a capitalist society is very different. It requires few skills and subordinates one to someone else's direction, forcing one to give up control over one's own activities. Alienation threatens because lives are largely taken up by activities in which one is forced, devalued, and dependent on the economic and often political power of others.

Humans differ from other animals in their ability to reflect about their lives and to change them according to the result of their reflections. Religious leaders summon us to a purer life devoted to God instead of materialistic enjoyments. Moral teachers exhort us to be ever mindful of our moral obligations and to live peacefully with our neighbors. Environmentalists urge us to change our patterns of consumption, and political leaders try to persuade us to adopt a variety of different political systems. All these admonitions presuppose the human capacity to devise new ways of life and actually adopt them. Marx refers to this ability of humans to remake their lives after rethinking them as our "species being": "The animal is one with its life activity. . . . But man makes his life activity itself an object of his will and consciousness" (Marx 1963:127). Capitalist wage work, he tells us, alienates us from this capacity to direct our lives in ways we have chosen for ourselves. Workers impoverished, oppressed by their employers, with very few opportunities for healthful leisure, for reflecting about their lives and altering those lives, cannot really participate in the human enterprise of thinking about the good life and making their lives conform to their ideas.

All of us are at the mercy of circumstances. We are alienated to the extent that we are unable to make our lives intelligible in spite of the forces that impinge on us. Alienation becomes more likely as the forces of circumstances become more powerful. Capitalism aggravates alienation because it puts wage workers in a position where their ability to give some coherence and meaning to their lives is seriously reduced. But capitalism also tends to intensify everyone's alienation because it transforms economic processes that could be under collective control, however tenuously at times, into quasi-natural processes that are said to be self-regulating: No human devices can resist their force so that they run roughshod over the goals and projects of individuals and groups. The often unexpected vagaries of the self-regulating market are just one more source of contingency depriving human beings of the possibility of directing and owning their lives. In a market society, Marx says (in the section of *Capital* that he titled "The Fetishism of Commodities and the Secret Thereof"), "the process of production has mastery over man, instead of being controlled by him" (1867:81). Thus the market alienates by setting us adrift on the sea of economic accidents. Socialism is attractive, Marx believed, because it allows human communities to try to tame the contingencies of economic processes and thus reduce alienation to some extent. (We shall return to this thought at the end of this book.)

Marx's very brief but very rich reflections about alienation are often boiled down to a few observations about social structures that oppress wage workers in a capitalist society.[1] Less attention is paid to Marx's suggestion that this oppression at work inhibits the ability of many persons to make their lives their own by choosing to live in one way rather than another. But the center of alienation is not the social or economic structure that oppresses; rather, it is the effect of that oppression on the personality that fails to develop its full powers to live a life of its own, to find meaning in that life and to make it worthwhile. By alienating us from our "species being"—our capacity to reflect on and reform our lives—the capitalist society reduces the scope of what is most human in our lives. Alienation distances us from lives all our own, transforming us into virtual bystanders to our own experiences and actions. In this Marx agrees with Kierkegaard and Nietzsche. At the center of alienation stands the reduced ability to live one's own life. Alienation dehumanizes; it makes persons less human not because they are uneducated or lack good table manners, but because they have a very tenuous hold on their lives, which are instead dominated by accidental conditions.

There is much more to be said about the effects of capitalism on the lives of all of us. I shall return to this issue at length in Chapters 4 and 5.

Nietzsche

Friedrich Nietzsche was born in Prussia in 1844, the son of a Protestant minister. The father died when Nietzsche was quite young and he was raised, together with his sister, by his mother, his grandmother, and two aunts. Early on he showed himself to be a brilliant student and, at only twenty-four years of age, became a professor of classics in Basel, Switzerland. Leaving his professorship in 1879, he spent the next ten years writing a number of books. In 1888 he suffered a nervous collapse from which he never recovered. He lived for ten more years, hopelessly insane. During the years before his collapse, he was plagued by migraines, stomach troubles, and a variety of other disabling disorders. He was also, in those years, a very lonely man.

Nietzsche provides this biting description of the alienated:

> The earth has become small and on it hops the last man. . . . "We have invented happiness" say the last men and they blink. They have left the regions where it is hard to live, for one needs warmth. One

still loves one's neighbor and rubs against him, for one needs warmth. Becoming sick and harboring suspicion are sinful to them: one proceeds carefully. . . . A little poison now and then that makes for agreeable dreams. . . . One still works, for work is a form of entertainment. But one is careful lest the entertainment be too harrowing. One no longer becomes poor or rich: both require too much exertion. . . . One shepherd, one herd! Everyone wants to be the same: whoever feels different goes voluntarily to the madhouse. . . . One has one's little pleasure for the day and one's little pleasure for the night: but one has regard for one's health. "We have invented happiness" say the last men and they blink. (Nietzsche 1954:129–130)

All of this is familiar. The alienated seek pleasure above all, and pleasure for them means living in a crowd, getting along, avoiding stress, effort, conflict. A caricature, to be sure, but one that captures familiar traits of everyday life in our world. Here there are no life projects; there is little in life that is terribly important beyond being comfortable. Everyone is the same; there is no individuality, no self. There is no concern with making one's life one's own. Getting along, staying out of trouble are of primary importance. The last men will buy anything that promises to make life easier, that is convenient, and that saves effort. For the rest, last men and women seek diversion, but nothing too strenuous, nothing stressful. The goal is to avoid stress, while keeping life interesting.

So far Nietzsche has described alienation in words similar to those used by Rousseau and Kierkegaard. But he enriches the, by now, standard depiction of alienation by developing an aspect of Dostoyevsky's picture of it. In *Notes from the Underground* the alienated are consumed by resentment. The extended soliloquy in *Notes* begins with "I am a sick man; I am a spiteful man," and the central character of that story is animated above all by jealousy, by resentment, and ill will. Ostensibly, resentment is directed against others—those with more money, more power, more friends. The alienated are resentful because their lives are difficult: Their lives do not hang together; it is not clear why they are doing anything. Torn by inner conflict, they are indecisive. They feel powerless; they lack autonomy and are to that extent under the control of other persons, or the accidental circumstances of their lives. Persons who are simply different arouse their resentment, as do people whose lives seem to be more coherent and happier, because the alienated suspect them of enjoying unfair advantages—How else could they be happy?—or of being "stuck up," because they lead lives of their own and stay away from crowds. But, in reality, this resentment of the alienated against others is a resentment against themselves, for being incompetent, in-decisive, unhappy (Nietzsche 1968:400). Self-hatred and self-denigration are central characteristics of alienation. The desire "not to be oneself," which Kierkegaard considers typical of alienation, comes back here in a more raw and emotional form as resentment against oneself. "If only I were someone else . . . but there is no hope of that. . . . And yet—I *am sick of my-self!* . . . [H]ere the worms of vengefulness and rancor swarm . . . " (Niet-zsche 1969:122). Resentment against others conceals self-hatred.

So far, too, Nietzsche deepens familiar views of alienation. With his doc-trine of the "will to power," he takes a passing observation of Rousseau's—namely, that those who manage to resist alienation have a "keen sense of living"—and gives it new depth. Nietzsche shows that those who manage to take a stand against alienation live to make their life and their persons their own. All of life, he tells us, is animated by the "will to power." That will does not primarily strive to dominate other persons but, rather, is a much more general striving to meet challenges, to overcome difficulties, to grow by doing what is hard, and to strengthen oneself by resisting the forces that threaten to dominate us. Will to power is that within us which resists: It "can manifest itself only where it encounters opposition; it, there-fore, seeks what will resist it—this is the original tendency of protoplasm when it extends its pseudopodia. . . . Appropriating and assimilation is above all a will to overcome, is shaping, forming, and transforming . . . " (Nietzsche 1968:346)

The will to power resists, whether that be sense-impressions when we concentrate and shut out distracting noise, or whether it be bodily needs for food or sleep that may divert us from our projects. Will to power allows us to brave criticism for living life as we see fit and to maintain our sense of self in the face of social pressure or hostility from those who see things differ-ently from us. Will to power allows us to take risks because we are able to weather failure and disappointment with our sense of self reasonably intact. In modern times, Nietzsche thought, the will to power is enervated. We are a feeble race who want comfort instead of challenges, convenience instead of difficulties to be overcome, relaxation instead of the tension that attends cre-ation (Nietzsche 1968). In the alienated the will to power is feeble.

We live in a world imperfectly understood and controlled by us, the tenor of our lives determined by a body and personality not of our own choosing. Our striving for a life of our own, directed to goals we have chosen, our desire for freedom and self-determination, is from the very be-ginning compromised. Unexpected events deflect us from our path and force us to make new plans or invent new projects for ourselves. We must be resilient and able to resist in order to live in this world as our own persons, and some are better able to do that than others. Some will get up after a fall, shake off the dust, and pursue their goals; others are left prostrate and discouraged, their sense of their own competence and worth sapped by every unhappy event that they had no reason to expect and little strength to resist. Some are like Nietzsche's Zarathustra, independent, cheerful in the face of loneliness and deprivation, unperturbed by events and never deflected from pursuing the sort of life that their nature demands. Others are "last men."

Zarathustra, as portrayed in Nietzsche's major work *Thus Spoke Zarathustra*, is "will to power" personified. He has lived in the mountains by himself for ten years and now returns to civilization to teach his fellow human beings about the good life. Zarathustra is independent; his life is his own. He does not need love or friends. All he wants are disciples with whom to share the overflowing insights he has gathered in his ten years of solitude on a mountaintop. He owes nothing to anyone else; his ideas have not been elaborated in conversation with others; his sense of himself does not require recognition by others. He feels secure without being loved. He is unaffected by the opinions of other people, or by what others think "one" should be doing. Zarathustra is bold, he is confident, he is cheerful, he affirms himself in his bearing and his actions. His bodily needs for food or sleep do not hold him back; Zarathustra is free. Others are debilitated by every mishap; even in good times their anxious anticipations of disasters prevent them from living exuberantly and going their own way. They cannot stand to be disapproved of; the slightest hint of criticism will have them running to change their ways for fear of finding themselves alone or ridiculed. Such are the "last men" who have long given up any hope for living lives of their own, who have no past and never think about the future. All they need is to be comfortable in the present, like terminal patients who want nothing more than that their pain be eased. They are consumed by resentment of those who depart from accepted norms; the slightest mishap will send them scurrying for safety because their sense of themselves is so fragile. Zarathustra is the very opposite of the "last men."

Why are we so different from Zarathustra? Why is our "will to power" so feeble? Why are we alienated? Nietzsche has a number of different answers to these questions. Inner strength, just like strength in the body, is acquired by practice and needs to be maintained. But in the world of the last men, what little strength remains is dissipated through disuse. When being relaxed, taking it easy, saving effort, and being comfortable are the supreme goals of life, few opportunities present themselves for making a life for oneself and resisting external influences—efforts that maintain or even increase one's strength. Life in the comfortable world of wealth enfeebles us. Alienation results from conditions of life—economic, according to Marx, and spiritual, according to Nietzsche. But alienation further debilitates us and thus intensifies itself. The situation becomes more serious as time goes on because, being alienated, we practice resistance less and less and thus progressively lose the ability to make our lives our own. Alienation is a progressive disease.

Nietzsche's central explanation of why we are alienated draws on an entirely imaginary history he concocted from his hatred of Christianity, a quasi-biological theory about racial decadence that was quite familiar to Nietzsche's nineteenth-century readers, and a dash of anti-Semitism. In this imaginary history, Nietzsche draws his own version of the "natural man," whom we already encountered in Rousseau, in order to explain why some of us are a bit like Zarathustra, and most of us like the last men. A long time ago—so goes Nietzsche's history of the human race—all humans were strong like Zarathustra. Then the earth was populated by "noble races," by "the splendid *blond beast* prowling avidly in search of spoil and victory" (Nietzsche 1969:40–41). Nietzsche's natural man is less benign than Rousseau's, but no less imaginary. His strength, his violence and brutality, Nietzsche claims, were tamed by a sinister conspiracy of priests—Jewish and Christian—and our weakness today is a sad testimonial to the destructive power of religion, of what we call morality and civilization. The strong have been emasculated through the machinations of the weak. Needless to say, that version of human history is worthless because it is not supported by evidence.

Also central to Nietzsche's story is his equation of this inner strength, the ability to resist the unexpected and often uncomprehended, with being independent from other people. Like Rousseau before him and like many contemporary philosophers, Nietzsche understood alienation as the lack of autonomy or self-determination. The autonomous person is his own master, beholden to no one, who needs no one and never wavers in the confidence in his powers and worth. The alienated, on the other hand, are conformists, dependent at every turn on the approval and affection of others. The strong, such as Zarathustra or the blond beast, are solitary persons and that is the secret of their strength. They need no one. Their ideas, their values, their projects are their own in a literal sense; they owe no one and need not feel gratitude to anyone.

This identification of strength, the ability to lead one's own life and to resist alienation, with being a solitary human being has a long history. It is still popular among philosophers who imagine themselves as the captains

of their ships and the masters of their soul. It is nevertheless in error, as we
shall see in detail in the next chapter.

Is Alienation Real?

Writers about alienation tend to assume that alienation is real, but not
everybody agrees with that. The reasons for taking the idea of alienation
seriously require some discussion.

Many philosophers believe that actions are good if they increase humanity's balance of pleasure over pain. We are to assess actions by asking
whether they contribute to human happiness by increasing pleasure. Such
a view does not encourage selfishness for it allows the individual to incur
greater pain him- or herself for the sake of increasing the total of human
happiness. Sacrifices made for others may hurt me but are noble if they
benefit others by filling their life with pleasure.

This doctrine, known as utilitarianism, has come under criticism for un-
dervaluing the rights of each separate individual. Utilitarianism, it is said,
allows us to injure individuals if that would increase total human happiness. But individuals, the critics insist, have a right not to be used to increase the happiness of the whole.

Writers about alienation are also critical of utilitarian doctrines, but for a
different reason: In the course of a lifetime we do many good things and
many good things happen to us, but it is a terrible mistake to call every one
of these goods "pleasures" because our goods are of very different kinds and
so are our experiences of them. It is impossible to think well about one's life
or about the lives of others, if "pleasure" is the name of all the many different values we pursue. A good meal, good sex gives me *pleasure*. Undertaking a difficult task and bringing it to a good conclusion may give me great
satisfaction. I take *pride* in overcoming difficulties. If sacrifices I make benefit
others I may derive some *comfort* from that. A life that makes sense inspires
me with a calm *cheerfulness*. If I live my life well, I hope that, at the end, I
may face death *serenely*. The help of a friend inspires me with *confidence;* I
learn to *trust* her love for me. A good conversation leaves me *animated,* and I
look forward to the visit of my children with *eager anticipation*. If a loved one
escapes danger I experience profound *relief;* if an important document,
which appeared to be lost, is found, my agitation is followed by *equanimity*.
Then I realize that I had misunderstood the actions of another, my feelings
of irritation disappear and my previous *affection* for the person returns. In
our lives we have very many different positive experiences, but it would be

a great mistake to call all of them "pleasures" because there are important qualitative differences between them.

In discussions of alienation, pleasure is implicitly held to be only one of many different positive feelings and experiences that all together make a good life. Pleasure alone is not enough. We need peace, pride in ourselves, satisfaction, cheerfulness, a sense of direction, trust in our friends and the world, and many other positive emotions and attitudes. One can reply, of course, that all of these different goods are but different pleasures and that therefore we should talk only about pleasure and pain. But that is a philistine suggestion to replace our rich and varied moral language with a blunt and unexpressive jargon that makes it impossible to talk intelligently about the good life.

All the authors discussed in this chapter make clear that the language to discuss what is good and bad in human life is much richer and more complex than utilitarianism would allow us. Ivan Ilych seeks pleasure above all. But, Tolstoy suggests, he misses the satisfaction derived from a trusting marriage. When his ceases to be fun, he leaves the house. He refuses to listen to his wife, who is pregnant and tearful. He misses out on the contentment that comes with being kind to persons he loves, and on the warmth between two persons who trust one another. We would not call either of these "pleasures," but they are important experiences nonetheless. There are many more important life experiences than those that are "pleasant and decorous." In similar ways, Kierkegaard extols the faithfulness of marriage partners and the quiet confidence one gains from knowing that one has kept one's promises and that one is a reliable person, in contrast to the unending pursuit of pleasure and the flight from boredom. Marx points to the difference between work that is unpleasant—because it is hard, or demanding, or repetitive—and work that, in addition, does not enhance one's competence and does not fill one with pride, does not earn one respect and admiration from others. Most work is tiring; often it is repetitive. But not all tiring and repetitive work alienates the worker. Sometimes we glory in activity, even though it brings us no intrinsic pleasure, because we can take pride in the accomplishment of it, as well as in our strength and skill. The question about work is not really whether it is pleasant or unpleasant; there is a great deal of unpleasant work that is nevertheless part of a good life: changing diapers, washing dishes, comforting a fussy baby at two in the morning. But the unpleasantness is nothing to the serenity one feels in holding this child. The experience cannot be called "pleasant" but it is profoundly valuable. Nietzsche makes similar observations. Strength, in the sense of being able to resist external forces, to shut out distractions, to allow one to overcome great sorrow, is of the essence of a good life. We need it if we are to make some sort of sense of the lives we have been given and that we live in the midst of many accidental influences. Talk about pleasure as the "unqualified good" conceals all these important needs for a good life and distracts us from reflecting usefully about the lives we need.

The question of whether alienation exists has to do with what are good things in human lives and what are not. Alienated lives are impoverished because pleasures and pains loom large while many other sustaining experiences are neglected and become unavailable in a world that dashes madly after pleasure and diversion. These are not matters capable of proof. One can put before the reader the different ways of viewing the world, and the different words used to articulate different experiences. But one cannot claim to have demonstrated, beyond the shadow of a doubt, that alienation exists. I know of no way to convince anyone of the multiplicity of valuable experiences and the poverty of a life devoted mainly to the pursuit of pleasure. One can only hope that sooner or later the doubters will see what they have missed.

A second controversy in this context acknowledges that the life of pleasure is just one of many, but then claims that the pursuit of pleasure is infinitely preferable to any other form of life. The calm performance of duty is said to be "boring" and the faithful cleaving to loved ones and friends only a sign of lack of imagination. Only rigid persons afraid of spontaneity would follow a life plan religiously. Only persons incapable of boredom would do the same sort of work year in and year out with unwavering faithfulness. That opinion, too, cannot be shown to be wrong; it cannot be refuted. But Kierkegaard exhibits convincingly the weaknesses of the single-minded pursuit of pleasure: Pleasures fade, repetition is the enemy, the search for new sources of entertainment and diversion continues but boredom is always just around the corner. The pursuit of pleasure easily ends in a depression.

Critics of alienation will argue that different persons have very different desires. "Who are you," they say, "to be critical of other persons' desires?" Some people just want to have fun; others want to think deeply about their lives and make sure that they have meaning. All persons are entitled to their own senses of what theirs lives are about. But defenders of alienation will point out that we often desire what, later, we discover to have been really bad for us. The woman I loved so passionately turns out to have been so different from me that it would have been impossible for us to share our lives happily. I turn out to have no aptitude for the world that I had expected to be creative and interesting; I do it badly and am left feeling inadequate. Our desires are often mistaken; they are definitely open to criticism. The same is true of everyone's desires, and the errors of the other are often more obvious to us than our own.

"Life has no meaning," many critics of alienation tell us—and, with that, begins another long conversation about human lives. Are they all equally empty and pointless? Are some not preferable to others? The grounds for the rejection of alienation as a serious philosophical concept are often flimsy. It is not as obvious as some self-styled realists believe that alienation is an empty idea. The ubiquity of alienation is not self-evident, either. The invitation, offered in this book, to reflect seriously about alienation—including its very existence—is no more than an invitation to think seriously about the life one is living.

Summary

Rousseau, Kierkegaard, Marx, and Nietzsche add a great deal to the weight of evidence in favor of the reality of alienation. It is difficult to read their works seriously without being convinced that alienation is a genuine problem in human lives. What emerges clearly from this history of the concept of alienation is the idea that the alienated are not themselves; they have difficulties with being a person in their own right and with living a life that is their own. Lacking a self of one's own, one tends to have low self-esteem and to be filled with resentment. Depression also is often a symptom of alienation—as is, under different circumstances, a frantic search for novelty, for pleasure, for the approval of others. These are important insights into alienation, but the key question of what it means not to be oneself does not receive a satisfactory answer in the traditional treatments of alienation. Not being oneself is not the same as being conformist; being utterly alone and isolated in the manner of a Zarathustra is not the same as resisting alienation. The more detailed explanation of what alienation is remains to be given. I will provide that in the next chapter.

Notes

1. For a particularly exhaustive version of this purely structural account of Marxist concept of alienation, see Arnold (1990).

3

ALIENATION
AND THE HUMAN CONDITION

The first chapter introduced the distinction between specific alienation, a widening distance that specific events and actions open between two or more persons, and global alienation, which affects a person much more broadly by putting a distance between her and her life. She feels powerless to shape that life; she says that it does not belong to her; it has no meaning. She is not herself and lacks a proper identity. But at the end of that first chapter we encountered a serious question: Are these complaints to be taken seriously? Not everyone believes that alienation is real because many regard it as a kind of intellectual or emotional hypochondria. This question received an answer in the second chapter from several outstanding philosophers.

Beginning with some common but inadequate ideas, this chapter explains what alienation is. Born into a world not of our own choosing and living lives buffeted by accidents, human beings are capable of being alienated because they, nevertheless, strive to give some sense to their existence. Human lives are profoundly ambiguous, between efforts to be self-directed and the overwhelming power of external forces. This ambiguity is the *precondition of alienation*. We can succumb to the ambiguity and be alienated or resist and try to give some sense to our lives. This struggle for mastery in one's life takes place in many different episodes, some of which this chapter discusses: work, love, the search for meaning, self-esteem. One can continue the effort to direct one's life if one has a solid sense of one's own worth derived largely from being recognized by other members of groups in which one works. Strong selves depend on their relationships to others, on mutual recognition.

Misunderstandings of Alienation

We now have good reasons to believe that alienation exists and that it matters a great deal, but what alienation is remains rather vague. Writers say over and over again that the alienated are not themselves, but that is too general to be useful. In reflecting about my own life, how will I recognize that I am not myself? What are the symptoms of that condition?

More seriously, is it even possible for a person not to be him- or herself? How can anyone possibly not be oneself? Nothing seems more evident than that all things and persons are themselves and not something else. They may not be who we *think* they are, if we mistake their identity, but that identity, however misidentified, surely belongs to that person as firmly as anything. At the airport a stranger asks me whether I am Bill Peterson. I reply, "No, I am Richard Schmitt." He tells me that I look exactly like Bill Peterson, but that makes no difference because I have an unambiguous identity of my own, that of Richard Schmitt. Misidentifications are possible only because each of us is who he or she is.

In the effort to articulate our experience of alienation we keep wanting to say that we are not ourselves. But we know now that we cannot take that expression literally. The philosophical commonplace that the alienated are not themselves is clearly a metaphor, and that metaphor needs to be explained before we can understand our own alienation. This turns out to be a complex undertaking.

Metaphors about selves are commonplace in everyday speech. We ascribe to each person a self that, when young, one needs to find. When young persons are vague about their future they are told that they need to find themselves. At other times, we admonish them to be true to themselves. Polonius's advice to Laertes, in Shakespeare's *Hamlet*, "to thine own self be true," is still a staple of graduation addresses and parental counsel. Ordinary people are often accused of yielding to pressures to conform instead of being themselves. They are then condemned as "inauthentic" because authentic persons are themselves and resist pressures to adopt widely held opinions and expectations (Heidegger 1929). Often also the self is portrayed as a hard taskmaster, and if we fail to be ourselves we are blamed for being weak, lazy, or self-indulgent. Others speak of the self as a potentiality specific to each person that each must realize in order to become him- or herself. External circumstances, lack of requisite opportunities, or unwillingness to do the hard work required may thwart self-realization, and thus one goes through life as an inadequate, failed version of the person one might have been. One falls short of being oneself.

It is often very convenient to speak of a self that we look for, or are true to, or that we manage to realize. It is also very tempting to understand alienation as a disturbance of this special part of persons, the self. The alienated are then thought not to be that self, to have failed in realizing it. They are said to be "estranged" from it. One scholar ascribes to Marx the doctrine that the alienated have not achieved their "real nature" (Popitz 1968), and another thinks that Marxian alienation has to do with failure to realize oneself (Peffer 1990). However much alienation may be affected by social conditions, it is ultimately a private drama played out within persons who are less than their real self because they cannot realize it.

However convenient such familiar ways of speaking, they must be understood as shorthand expressions for much more complicated thoughts. Literally speaking, all are who they are, each is him- or herself. You can no more not be yourself than you can take a train on platform 9¾ at King's Cross Station (Rowling 1998). Many writers are therefore rightly suspicious of this supposed real self from which alienation separates us. That self which the alienated are said not to realize seems too much like a convenient fiction. Instead of appealing to this questionable fabrication, Rousseau, Tolstoy, Nietzsche, and others explicate alienation as conformism—the unwillingness to live one's own life, subordinating oneself instead to whatever everyone else thinks. The self the alienated lack is not a distinct entity but, rather, a shorthand expression for a set of choices one makes with respect to the demands of one's social environment. One is said to not "be oneself" or to not be living "one's own life" if one allows others to shape one's way of life and thoughts.

This is a plausible view of alienation and has been held by a number of thinkers, but we have already seen that such conformism is not so easy to understand either. Humans are social through and through; not only are we born helpless and formed into human beings by many social influences but, upon reaching adulthood, our identity depends on social roles, on social relationships, on doing our work the way it is done in this society. In every act, in every gesture, in what we say, in what we wear, in what we eat—everywhere our society makes itself felt. It is impossible to detach ourselves from the pervasive influence of social custom. Yes, some persons are excessively influenced by their surroundings. But when do prevailing practices and conceptions affect us too much, or when does the influence of social custom become extreme? An interesting question, and an important one, but not one to which an answer is ready at hand. Conformism is no easier to understand than alienation. In order to understand alienation more precisely, we need to explain how the influence of others may rob us of our identity.

As we have noted, human beings are social through and through. But when is our reliance on others excessive? Philosophers have used the concept of autonomy to answer that question. Conformism, they tell us, is the failure to be autonomous. Men and women are autonomous if they think for themselves, if their ideas are their own, or if they borrow ideas from others only after having examined them carefully and finding them acceptable.

They are autonomous if they live according to life plans that they have adopted for themselves, if they live by moral rules they have chosen to follow, and are independent, self-determining, and in charge of their lives (Schmitt 1995: ch. 1 and pp. 45ff.). Philosophers, predominantly male, have propounded this portrait of the autonomous man for a long time.

This prevailing philosophical story about autonomy is, however, not defensible. Sometimes autonomy is characterized as living by one's own moral rules (Benn 1975–1976). But Dostoyevsky's Raskolnikov lived by his own moral rules and murdered an old woman pawnbroker after persuading himself that murder was justified if it allowed one to do a greater good. Making up one's own rules commonly results in flagrant immorality, not in being one's own person. Morality belongs not to individual persons but to groups who develop moral standards in the course of elaborate discussions about right and wrong and the good life. These discussions go on in churches, in schools, in families, among friends, in newspapers, in the political arena. Just think of the continuing debates about abortion, euthanasia, the death penalty, drug use, child labor, environmental destruction. Moral rules are the accomplishments of groups and are shared by their members. A personal morality is an impossibility.

Other philosophers, trying to characterize autonomy, stress the importance of living one's life according to freely chosen life plans, ignoring completely the contingency in human lives. But this notion brings us no closer to an understanding of autonomy. If the world cooperates and allows one to follow one's plan without incident, there is little challenge; one is just plain lucky that everything works out as planned, and that hardly constitutes autonomy. But most plans are again and again disrupted by unforeseen disasters, by war, floods, earthquakes, traffic accidents, or assaults in the street. Being oneself has more to do with being able to carry on one's life in some sort of coherent fashion even if major catastrophes have nullified all plans. One's life is one's own to an extent if one manages to create a measure of continuity in spite of many plans derailed by unforeseen events. Doggedly following one's life plan, made in times of peace and prosperity, while war and famine ravage the land is being not autonomous but rigid and insensitive to the suffering of others. It is plain foolish to turn one's back on extraordinary luck—winning the lottery, finding a lover, being offered an unexpected opportunity—because it does not fit in one's life plan.

Independence is often cited as an essential component of autonomy. But the desire for independence may well signify lack of a firm self. The more fragile the self, the more dependence on anyone appears as a threat because one feels in danger of being swallowed up by the other. Children, their selves still fragile, must contradict their parents in order to be themselves. Adults should have overcome such childish self-doubt and be able to accept the ideas of others—as in fact they do most of the time, for none of us can honestly claim to have reflected deeply on every belief we have. Adults should be able to acknowledge their intellectual dependence on others without needing to pretend that they are not beholden to anyone for their ideas. Being oneself, on the contrary, allows one to accept help, to receive love and friendship without feeling burdened, or threatened with loss of identity. Being oneself, as we shall see below, is to be closely connected to other persons (see the section below titled "Recognition"). The powerful urge to be independent is rarely a mark of the person who is fully him- or herself. Neither do the truly independent need to hold views all of their own.

Alienation, being estranged from oneself, remains an unclear idea. There exists no single entity—a self all one's own—from which the alienated are separated. It is difficult to give a clear interpretation of the idea that alienation consists of being under the undue influence of cultural norms or shared beliefs because we are social beings through and through and are shaped by the ideas of others as well as by customs. It is not an easy matter to decide when social influences are excessive. Finally, alienation is not lack of autonomy, as that idea is commonly understood, because such autonomy is either undesirable, or impossible, or the mark of a fragile personality. Explaining alienation turns out to be quite difficult.

Alienation and Its Precondition

Alienation is, to some extent, different in each life. One can understand it only if one is willing to consider specifics, to tell particular stories and reflect about them. Philosophers rarely do that because philosophy is very abstract. Philosophical discussions of alienation, therefore, suffer from excessive generality. Two novels will help us overcome that difficulty.

The story of John Dufresne's (1997) *Love Warps the Mind a Little* is soon told. Lafayette Proulx, born to French-Canadian working-class parents in Worcester, Massachusetts, meets Martha while studying at Worcester State. They fall in love and marry. Sixteen years later, Laf starts an affair with a therapist, Judi Dubey, and in an exalted moment tells Martha about it. She kicks him out of the house; Judi somewhat reluctantly takes him in. When, a few months later, Judi is diagnosed with ovarian cancer, Laf faithfully nurses her through her final illness. A kind of love that neither of them had known before grows up between them and, at the end of the story, Laf is a bit stronger and his life less adrift.

Laf is interesting because, being a writer, he is trying to make sense of his and others' lives. He is continually telling himself stories, not all of which get written down, that reflect on his own life, and that of others. These stories respond to the ever-present threat of alienation, of life without any meaning, by illuminating actual or possible meanings in different lives. But as Laf understands it, meaninglessness, alienation, has little to do with adopting a life plan, or choosing moral values, or having one's own ideas. The need for infusing one's life with meaning arises, as Kierkegaard understood, through the duality of human life. We are, after all, animals, governed by instinct and habit; but we also plan and think; our lives seem utterly swayed by blind accident and yet we try to make them into something that has an intelligible story. Laf understands the ambiguity of the human condition. With our situation in tension, stretched as we are between brute animality and purposive reasoning, we want to but are not fully able to lead meaningful lives of our own choosing. Profoundly ambiguous, our humanity impels us toward a life we cannot always lead. Telling stories is one way of confronting this ambiguity of human life. "The difference between fiction and life is that fiction makes sense" (p. 46).

One's relation to the body exemplifies this ambiguity. Human bodies are subject to unexpected diseases, as are the bodies of all animals. As Judi's cancer is being removed surgically, Arthur, a meat cutter, complains about the tumors he finds in diseased steers at the packing plant (p. 163). The grim parallel between the steer being cut up and the woman undergoing an operation is inescapable. Our bodies are animal bodies; but what, Judi ponders, as she is dying, is our relation to our bodies? "Am I my cancer?" she asks herself, or is it just something I have? Her body's illness kills her; it is the body that makes us mortal. At the very center of our life is this power, the body, that we can affect but do not control. A person is more than her body, because she chooses how to react to and how to live with the body and with mortality. Often our bodies override our choices; they seem, to Laf, to have lives of their own (p. 85). The body provides tools for the mind: Fingers type out the words of a book. If the brain is foggy from drink or disease, so is the mind—now mind and body seem to be the same entity rather than tool and user. Sometimes a severely debilitated body does not impair the quality of a person's mind, which seems now quite distinct and superior to the suffering body. The ambiguous relations of minds and bodies give the lie to any idea we might have about controlling our lives. For Judi, the relation to Laf promises to end her previous pattern of having relations to married men or men otherwise committed. She is growing into being her own person. Then she falls ill and dies. Her body has the last word.

Bodies are our presence in the world and with other persons. We are known, in part, because we are seen, touched, smelled by others. Our bodies are given to us; we do not choose them. But it makes a great deal of difference to one's life whether one is born white or black, male or female; whether one is large or small, strong or weak. Yet one's appearance obviously is not completely outside one's control. My presence in the world is a given that I need to learn to live with, but not quite. One can make different uses of one's appearance. Richie, a member of Judi's extended family, is a very large man. He is also very violent and uses his extraordinary size to signal that he is dangerous. Another person might well make a very different use of his unusual size by being gently protective of others as he helps them. There are very different ways to be a man or a woman and we have some choice over how to live in these bodies, just as we can choose to live out our lives as whites or blacks in different ways. Bodies determine our lives, but not completely.

Bodies make us into sexual beings. We have no choice in that respect. We can repress our sexuality (or try to) but we cannot get rid of it. As our bodies are not transparent to us, neither is our sexuality and we often use it in ways that we do not understand at the time. Laf, for instance, is very conflicted about his marriage. He and Martha loved each other when they got married; he still loves her. At the same time, strains are beginning to show between them. Martha is not supportive of his plan to become a full-time writer. She wants him to continue teaching high school English so that they can save for their retirement, buy a home, and, generally, be financially secure. Laf is content to work part time at the "Our Lady of the Sea Fish and Chips" eatery and to spend the rest of his days writing stories and doggedly sending them out to other magazines after they have been rejected. In Martha's eyes he is being utterly irresponsible; to him, he is doing what he most wants to do. Laf worries whether his starting an affair with Judi was a way of forcing an issue in his life that he had not yet been consciously willing to confront. Was his sexuality moving him toward a major change in his life while he was not yet ready to consider it? Sexuality is an independent force that controls human lives more often than they control it. Like the body in general, it is not always understood by us; sexuality acts on and for us when we do not know it.

Through our bodies we are inserted into a world. The body mediates between us and that world. We perceive the world through our senses. But what is it we see, and what shall we make of what we perceive? Different lives have different realities. Judi's father, a kindly, harmless schizophrenic, believes that his single-handed efforts protect the world against the forces of evil. But he admits, in his more lucid moments, that he escaped into schizophrenia after the suicide of his oldest son. Some versions of reality are crazy. But which ones? Judi, a bright and insightful psychotherapist, believes firmly that she can remember previous existences and that she continues, in her present life, stories begun in earlier ones. Martha is the secretary for the Catholic bishop in Worcester and believes in the trinity and transubstantiation. Laf does not believe in much of anything, but his story telling is, of course, his way of creating his reality. In his world, people have lives that make sense because they make interesting stories. Different persons, different lives, different realities. Reality is made as well as given, and being oneself involves negotiating one's reality.

We are born into particular families. Laf's working-class family and friends are suspicious of his writing. They do not really know what being a writer entails and suspect that he is just being lazy. He does not, they think, want to have a family, to hold down a job, or maybe two, to make a living and raise his kids. Had Laf's parents been college professors and their friends writers and artists, there would have been a lot more encouragement for him and a lot more help with getting anything published. Laf is very different from his family. His parents and brother live in Florida, and he has not really talked to them for fifteen years. His brother is his very opposite—a charismatic Catholic who owns a *Pollo Tropico* franchise in Boca Raton and never thinks about anything. But this family is nonetheless part of Laf's world; in making sense of his life he needs to find a place for them in his story. Judi's family is, by any standard, dysfunctional—there is suicide, addiction, criminality, and plain madness. Your family, Judi says at one point, is a part of who you are. It is another aspect of your life that is chosen for you but you also have to make something of it (p. 198).

Alienation is a threat in human lives because we live as persons we did not choose to be in a world not of our own making. We did not choose our bodies, or our minds, or our emotional life. The families we are born into play important roles in our lives, even if we are distant from them as adults. But these lives, bodies, families that are given to us are not ours, they just happen to us. This life I lead is purely fortuitous and, therefore, without meaning. To the extent that my life is given and not owned—as soldiers' uniforms are issued to them and remain property of the government—to the extent that what happens in my life is determined by forces outside of myself, my life is not my own. It just happens; it doesn't mean anything. There is no point in asking what my life is good for because it is just a series of random events.

Because we are *geworfen* (thrown) into this world, we do not know it and that only intensifies the *strangeness* of the world, even as it appears most familiar. We find ourselves in the world, as we grow up, and need to discover its traits. We are not born understanding the world, nor do we know who we are ourselves but must discover that as life goes on. Even old people, after a lifetime of becoming familiar with their own nature, will surprise themselves when they experience emotions of which they had thought themselves incapable, or when they find themselves doing what they had been certain they would never do. In many situations one is not sure what one is feeling. One's emotions are by no means transparent. They do not come labeled as "anxious" or "fearful," and often one looks to others to confirm that one is happy. The narrator in Walker Percy's *The Moviegoer* observes this:

> The times we did have fun, like sitting around the fire or having a time with some girls, I had the feeling they were saying to me: "How about this, Binx? This is really it, isn't it, boy?," that they were practically looking up from their girls to say this" (Percy 1998:41).

His friends need him to confirm that they are having a good time, even in the midst of their love making, because feelings are not easily identified. We know our world, including ourselves, so imperfectly that we constantly need others to confirm our perceptions.

It is often difficult to decide what to do in a given situation. By trying things out, Laf quite gradually discovers that he is ready to leave Martha. He suspects that starting an affair with Judi was the beginning of untangling his complicated feelings for Martha and the role that marriage played in his life. What was he doing when he caught Judi's eye in a singles' bar? What was he doing, a man married sixteen years to a woman he loved (or thought he loved?), going into a singles' bar in the first place? Did he just happen to go into a bar that turned out to be a singles' meeting place? Was he "just looking"? Perhaps looking for a one-night stand? The questions are endless, and answers scarce. At times we find ourselves doing something that surprises us and we ask ourselves: "Where did that come from?" Much of our person is hidden from us until it makes us act in ways that surprise us. Laf often feels manipulated by his unconscious (p. 63).

We do not know the world at birth and we do not know ourselves by self-inspection. Making sense of our life includes finding out what situations we are in, what they mean, and what we are willing and able to do about them. We are not just disembodied thinking beings but find ourselves in material worlds we must explore, learn to know, and interpret. We also need to come to know ourselves. These voyages of discovery often begin with acting, quite tentatively, in order to see what reaction one will get from others, as well as from oneself. Making sense of one's life is finding out where one is, as what person. We are shuffling in the dark, our hands held out in front, trying to guess where and who we are. Unlike fiction, life does not make ready-made sense.

Laf's dog, Spot, does not worry about the opacity of the world in which he finds himself. He just happily chomps away at sticks, newspapers, and other chewables. He woofs when someone says "spot" (as in "You have a spot on your shirt") and gets excited when Laf seems about to take him for a walk. The dog acts mostly on instinct or to satisfy momentary impulses. Alienation is not a feature of Spot's world but it is of Laf's—and ours— because we not only act in the world but we *think* about what to do and how to do it. We do not automatically chase any squirrels we see even though they are much too fast for us. Sometimes, at least, we think first and act afterward, and thus accustom ourselves to thinking about the world as we make our way in it. We consider life as a whole and inquire about its unity and its direction. We raise questions about its worth and ask why it is often so painful. We talk about good lives and lives that have been wasted. Imperfectly known to ourselves, in a world by no means transparent, we nevertheless try to tell a story that makes our life intelligible and meaningful.

This is the human condition: being minds embodied, rational beings caught in a world not of our choosing that is, much of the time, as opaque to us as is our own person. The foregoing is also the *precondition of alienation.* Different persons respond to this precondition in very different ways. Some, like Emma Bovary, whom we will meet in the next chapter, struggle valiantly against the ambiguities of human existence but fail to make their persons their own, or to give their lives some sense. Some avoid the struggle altogether by keeping thought to a minimum, going wherever life takes them, and trying to make it as pleasant for themselves as they can. They may grumble, but it does not occur to them to try to change their condition or themselves. Some leave thinking to others by doing what is expected of them and living mostly by imitation. Some escape into religious beliefs as if to say: "Yes, the world makes no sense, but that's OK. It's supposed to be a mystery." Thus Laf's brother Edmund, because the labor of trying to make sense of life is too daunting, becomes a charismatic Christian. Others just give up. They work; in between, they try to have fun. Judi's family lives in an old Quonset hut in the next town over. Her mother is energetically optimistic; until Judi's last moments, she denies that Judi is dying. Her sister Stoni, a nurse, pops any kind of pill that will get her high. Weekend parties, the respite from a week of work, are boozy, stoned-out-of-their-minds events. But Stoni is not happy. Kierkegaard would have said that she is in despair. Her life is fundamentally tedious and uninteresting. She tries to create some excitement by being engaged to Richie, the violent biker, and, while he is in prison, going out with Arthur, the meat cutter. Then Richie gets out of jail she continues her relations with both of them, even though both are very dangerous men. She is fortunate that neither kills her; instead, Arthur murders Richie and hangs him up in the slaughterhouse by his Achilles tendons like one more slaughtered steer.

Stoni's life is pointless, Laf thinks:

> The Dubeys [Judi's family] did not believe that life was purposeful. It was, rather, a situation to be endured. It helped if there were clever and/or amusing distractions about, which could take your mind off the emptiness. If they had been born into money, the Dubeys would all be out at the country club this afternoon, diverting themselves with games and chitchat about cars and real estate, and the world would think they were all productive and sensible. (p. 86)

Laf's mother refuses to emerge even for a moment from behind the mundane details of running the motel she and Laf's father own in Florida. When Laf comes to visit she notices only that he needs a haircut. More serious questions about what anyone is doing, or the fact that her husband is dying, are studiously avoided. Life is reduced to brief, small events, one following the other without much of any connection between them; and that, as far as she is concerned, is all there is.

This is alienation: evading the ambiguities of the human condition or being defeated by them. One flees into religious orthodoxy or diversions, into rigid optimism, into ambition, competition, violence, into unbending fixation on the small and insignificant details of life in order to overlook and pass by everything that is ambiguous, requires interpretation, cannot be well understood, let alone managed or changed, and leaves one perplexed and anxious. One indulges in heroic or romantic fantasies in order to distract oneself from one's real life and its demands and challenges. The precondition of alienation, of being thinking animals, is given. But alienation—giving up on making sense of one's life, providing it any direction at all—is, in some sense, chosen. One can, like Laf and Judi, work at living a life that is not utterly random; or one can just ignore the issue of meaning, as do Judi's and Laf's families, each in their own ways; or one can try to make a coherent story of one's life and fail. But the struggle against the precondition of alienation is much more difficult for some people than for others. Some lives are too burdened by external conditions for there to be any real choice of making it at all different. (In the next chapter I will discuss some circumstances that make it more difficult to resist the threat of alienation.)

A *second sense* of alienation flows from the first. Alienation, the evasion of our fundamental condition, suspended between animal and human, between body and spirit, leaves us discouraged, frightened, without any particular reason for continuing except that, as animals, we instinctively fear death. This is Kierkegaard's "despair," the *felt* misery of aimless lives, lives in which one is a faintly bewildered bystander, bored much of the time but occasionally amused. It is our animal nature that keeps us going with a project that, from a human perspective, is not "purposeful but, rather, a condition to be endured" (Dufresne 1997:86).

Alienation and Specific Life Tasks

We do not know yet how, precisely, to explicate the metaphor of being, or not being, oneself that is so tempting to use in trying to explain what alienation is. But we have moved ahead toward clarifying what alienation is, and what it means not to be oneself: Alienation consists of denying the profound ambiguity of human existence, or pretending that one has overcome it. One can make an effort to try to understand one's life, one's person, and one's condition, and try to lead a life that makes some sense under the conditions in which one finds oneself, or one can evade the ambiguities and perplexities and live from day to day, more or less oblivious to how one's life unfolds. But lives cannot be given meaning once and for all; there is no substitute for meeting each new day, and each unexpected situation or surprising discovery about oneself, and trying to domesticate its strangeness, or to break through its numbing familiarity. One can only try to make sense of oneself in specific conditions, facing concrete life tasks. In these various concrete situations we encounter tasks, to be taken on or evaded. One becomes oneself in the sequence of tasks taken on, or loses oneself as one task after the other is shirked. I will examine some of these tasks to see how each allows making life more intelligible. But each also leaves openings for evasions, for reinforcing alienation.

Choosing One's Life's Work

Most people work, usually in order to provide the necessities of life, but often also for the sheer satisfaction of working. Work is usually thought of as an activity that earns one money, such as cooking in a restaurant or taking care of small children or of old people. But if the cook comes home and prepares meals for his family, or puts his children to bed, that same activity is no less work because he does not receive a paycheck to reward him. Work involves significant expenditures of energy, whether it earns a wage or not. Some choose work that brings in no money when they volunteer for work that needs doing, or they choose badly paid work because they prefer that work regardless of what it pays. It is the activity that is essential to work, not the money it earns us.

Laf has chosen to be a writer. But has he really chosen that, or should we rather say that writing has chosen him? A life of one's own includes choosing work for oneself, but Laf's experience shows that choice to be less straightforward than we might have thought at first. Often one chooses work to fit with one's abilities, but one receives those at birth; one does not make those. What is good work for someone is, in the end, not chosen, but depends in large part on the talents one discovers in oneself as one grows up. Laf's contribution to his choice of work is his determination to become a professional writer in spite of the fact that, in his environment, that is an implausible choice. He does not, properly speaking, choose his life's work; he invests energy in an occupation chosen for him by his personality and abilities. The incredulity of those around him stands in his way, but so does his lack of self-knowledge, a condition that afflicts us all. For he is, of course, taking a chance. Perhaps his writing really is not very good and he will have wasted a great deal of time should he finally have to accept that. One takes a risk choosing one's life work because one knows so little about oneself and discovers what one can do mostly by trying it out.

Still, Laf chooses his work more explicitly than most. Most people leave college and find work that is of more or less interest to them. Then they marry and have children. Now they have mortgages, car payments, medical bills, and bills for clothes, toys, and school. So they stay in the job, but accident has played a significant role in who they came to be in this work. Or perhaps a student attracts the attention of a biology prof who, because he thinks well of her, suggests that she go to graduate school. She follows his advice and a few years later faces a large freshman biology class to whom she must explain the intricacies of genetics. Did she choose her work or slide into it? The answer is not clear. The choice of work is not a simple matter; it is not like choosing one flavor of ice cream over another.

Choosing work carefully would seem to be a way of trying to resist the precondition of alienation by finding in one's worklife a guiding thread to one's existence. Whatever else may happen to render life opaque and unpredictable, as long as I can, for instance, be a lawyer or a doctor I have a steady occupation that gives my life some continuity. But having the same job for a long time does not give meaning to one's life. That work may be just an external characteristic, such as having the same address or the same kind of haircut, while one lives one's life quite randomly without giving it any thought. The unchanging profession is only a means for evading the precondition of alienation by enabling one to live heedlessly, more or less from day to day, without asking oneself what one is doing and why. Some persons' choice of work is primarily determined by the fear of boredom; since they need to earn money in some way, they choose temporary work. Changing their workplace and occupation fairly often may be as deliberate a choice as taking up a professional career for their entire worklife. They choose variety in work in order to keep themselves amused. The opposite choice is probably more common: One commits oneself to a career in order to still all questions about who one is, what one's life is meant to be. To the question, Who am I? one can respond by saying: I am a teacher, a lawyer, a doctor. Needless to say, that is as much a case of evading the tasks of life as not having any very steady work, because the person who says "I am a teacher" has not told us yet what *kind* of teacher he is. Being a teacher, in general, is not an identity; only being this particular kind of teacher answers the question, Who am I? In both situations, one evades the pressing question about how one's life is developing, and how one can make it one's own life.

Some people would refuse certain sorts of work such as being a hired killer, selling drugs to schoolchildren, or running a house of prostitution. Taking some kinds of work or refusing others, if offered, implies choices of what sort of person one is to become. Not setting any limits to what one will do to earn money is also making a choice about what one will be— perhaps one who will do anything for money, if only there is enough of it. But work choices are not transparent and often bring challenging surprises. A successful law student is rewarded for her hard work with a job in a well-known firm and begins her career making a very large salary. But then she is assigned the defense of a major corporation that, in order to satisfy the greed of its stockholders, has done serious harm to its customers and to the environment. This very difficult dilemma, between defending corporate evildoers or quitting a prestigious and very remunerative job, affects the self. Will the lawyer choose money and prestige over what she had thought were firmly held moral principles? Will she say, in later years, that she was very idealistic when young but then quickly learned that one must make compromises, meaning that she goes where the money is best? Here is a choice of what sort of person she will be. One may agree with her choice or not, but she does choose to develop in one direction or another and thereby gives her life and her personality a definite shape. She takes a hand in becoming a certain kind of person and forming a definite sort of identity. But she can, of course, also evade the dilemma altogether by becoming cynical and refusing to consider her choices at all seriously, accepting or rejecting clients more or less on a whim, choosing what seems fun or challenging at the moment. In this manner she denies the precondition of alienation and the possibility of making herself into one kind or person rather than another. If she can be said to choose at all, she chooses drift and a personality that remains vague in important respects.

Choosing work does not always make one a person in one's own right. It may also be a means for evading the issue of alienation, of being oneself. In one's work, one may strengthen one's identity but one may equally well refuse to consider alienation at all. Obviously, however, not all people have the same opportunities to choose their work. For some, who have money and are well connected, the world is open to choose as they please. Others, whose opportunities are not as ample, need to do the first thing that comes their way just to keep body and soul together. The opportunities to resist the ambiguities of human existence are distributed very unevenly within societies. Moreover, entire societies differ from one another inasmuch as some make the resistance a lot more difficult than others. Culture and society contribute to the spread of alienation. (see Chapter 4).

Being Oneself

To hear philosophers talk, everyone has an actual self he needs to be at one with or a potential one that she needs to actualize. But actual lives are not as conveniently of one piece as this description suggests. Here is Laf's wife, Martha, who craves security, order, and a fairly conventional life, but she also rereads *Anna Karenina* every year and in her fantasies is a romantic heroine devoted to the man who has swept her off her feet. Many of us have multiple selves. Members of groups forced to the margins of society need to acknowledge that they are Americans (or Germans, or French), but just as much as that they are excluded because they are African-Americans, or Chicanos (or Turks, or Martinicans). The tension between belonging to the dominant culture and being excluded from it is so central to these lives that they cannot make sense unless the tension is acknowledged (Anzaldúa 1987). Comparable tensions beset many lives. Consider the computer expert who, during the day, thrives in a technological culture that rests on the confidence that new technologies can resolve most problems. But when he comes home he dons his work clothes to labor in his large garden of organic fruits and vegetables. To avoid the use of pesticides—a technological solution to the problem of plant diseases—he patiently picks the insects off his green beans and his potato plants. He lives in two worlds that are at odds with each other. Being oneself does not mean that one is all of one piece, free from tensions or activities that conflict with other practices. It does require, however, that one have some satisfactory account of the different sides of one's person, the different sorts of things one does, that often are quite inconsistent with each other.[1]

To be a writer one needs to be accepted by publishers, by readers, and by critics as a literary talent. To be a certain sort of person, one presents oneself to others as that person and needs them to accept one as one presents oneself. If Martha, the methodical, reliable, soft-spoken secretary to the bishop suddenly acted the passionate, spontaneous romantic heroine, which she also is, or at least would like to be, the quiet nuns sitting demurely in the foyer, waiting to speak to the bishop, would be bewildered and so would everybody else in the diocesan office. (She might, of course, find a different social setting where she is known only as a small-town Anna Karenina.) Living in the world, we need to manage the different persons we are. We need to be clear about what is fantasy and what is a game, what is more or less pretense to be other than one knows oneself to be. The fluctuations in one's identity have to be moderate so that others can recognize us from day to day and know us for who we are as public persons. Being oneself is not being literally one and the same person but is the much more complex project of managing the different persons one might be so that one can present a comprehensible persona to the world.

Human beings are not born coherent; more likely we find ourselves with inclinations that are not always compatible or abilities that conflict with each other. These multiplicities must be managed. Sometimes, however, they are not found by us in order to be managed but are created by us more or less deliberately in order to accommodate intolerable tensions in one's life. Pat Barker's *The Eye in the Door* (Barker 1995), a novel about British soldiers in World War I, explores in complex detail the ways in which the tension between being a skillful killer—the requirements for a good soldier—and being a decent human being forces various characters to develop quite different personalities to fit the different roles that are required of them and that they require of themselves. One coherent person cannot fill both roles because they are utterly contradictory. In a world that makes no sense because it makes incoherent demands on us, we respond by developing incompatible personalities to fit the different situations in which we regularly find ourselves (Schmitt 1990). Being oneself, in that situation, is not being one coherent person but being those different persons without allowing such conflicts to destroy oneself by driving one mad.

I may well be a different person in each of the different groups to which I belong. Talking to my neighbors about filling the potholes in our street or cleaning the trash from the sides of the pond, I am not quite the same person as I am in the thick of a discussion of Hegel's dialectic with fellow philosophers. The self gains content from the different projects undertaken together with others. The identity of individuals is intimately connected with their membership and the role they play in specific groups. The janitor at work is not quite the same person as the deacon in church on Sunday; the judge on the bench is not the same as the man reading a bedtime story to his child at night. The differences derive from the place occupied in these different groups. At work, the janitor is regarded and treated very differently from the deacon in church and yet they are the same person. The judge on the bench may be respected; he is certainly feared. At night, reading to his child, he is not feared for the power he has as a judge; he is loved. Personal identities are intimately connected with memberships in groups.

Managing one's different selves gives one an opportunity to bring some conscious order into a life. But it also allows one to have no sensible story at all about the different selves one is and how they are all connected. It is only too easy to be different persons in different parts of one's life but to pay no attention to that. Those parallel selves just have to coexist however they can. The liberal academic who works on the causes of a conservative political party for the prestige it brings may deny that he has a problem. He may tell us that he is following a clear life plan and thus his life is in order. He denies that he has a problem with the coherence of his different lives. One can use the diversity of one's lives and personalities to forge some sort of unity, or one can ignore the tensions, or deny them importance. Being oneself allows one to impose some sort of coherence on one's life, or one may yield to accidental influences and let one's life unfold however it develops.

Thus the metaphor of being oneself refers to the different aspects of managing the different persons one is, or can be; but at other times, it has a different meaning. As we grow up and reach consciousness we discover what sort of body as well as what kind of personality, habits, and capabilities we have. But this body, character, and personality we find ourselves with are, after all, only possibilities. A particular kind of body, if it is beautiful, allows us to be a vamp or a faithful lover; one's particular sort of mind can be employed in developing destructive schemes of fiendish complexity, or to alleviate the suffering of persons caught in complicated difficulties. One is oneself to the extent that one develops, at least to some extent, the different possibilities one has by making deliberate choices rather than leaving the development of one's personal character to accidents and external forces. Having a self, in that sense, refers to the efforts, sometimes successful, that one has made to use the different possibilities opened by one's personality, capacities, bodily constitution, and so on. It is a matter not of developing one already prefigured identity but, rather, of creating some sort of structure of a personality from the many different persons one might be. It is, rather, a matter of appropriating (a favorite term of Nietzsche's), of making one's own the different traits with which one is born. One becomes oneself by taking some, very limited, responsibility over the persons one comes to be.

In a somewhat different sense, being oneself has to do with having some power in one's life. Alienation is frequently experienced as powerlessness; the alienated feel that they can do nothing. Their life does not respond to their direction; it just unfolds. One does not live such a life in which one has no efficacy; it is lived for one by impersonal forces and therefore it is not one's own. Without power in one's own life, one does not own one's person. Being powerless, bewildered, confused, and adrift are all forms of not being oneself. One comes to be oneself only to the extent that one is not totally an outsider to one's own life, that one is not totally incapable of living the life one wants.

Being oneself has, then, at least three different senses. It may refer to managing one's different personalities and presenting a reasonably clear person to the view of others. It may refer to the degree to which one manages to give direction to the development of one's personality and character. It may, finally, refer to the extent that one is not completely powerless in the conduct of one's own life. Obviously, those last two senses are interrelated.

Meaning

Many events in life make no sense whatsoever. The death of a beloved child, wars, famines, floods, and conflagrations cause great pain but cannot be explained or justified. The alienated accept such events as paradigmatic of all of life; they expect no sense, no continuity. Life for them is not going anywhere; there exist neither purposes or projects. When Gregor Samsa, in Kafka's *Metamorphosis,* wakes up to find that he has turned into a giant cockroach, he is unhappy but not surprised. The most bizarre event in his life is no more surprising than the most ordinary one because neither makes any sense. Necessity and contingency in human lives manifest themselves in unexpected events that we cannot explain. They mock our powers and display our helplessness. But they also challenge us to resist by making some sort of sense of our lives.

However unintelligible individual events are, life as a whole may have some sense if we can weave an intelligible story about it, if it is more than a concatenation of unrelated happenings. Since human lives are all different, so are the stories we tell, reflecting the connections we establish between the different periods of our lives, the different relationships we have, the different sorts of work we experience, and the different places where we live. Many life stories derive their meaning from life goals pursued for many years. Such goals are a good deal less definite than the life plans philosophers recommend to us. A life plan includes plans for education, the jobs one will seek, the sort of person one will marry, children, retirement, foreign travel. Goals are much more indefinite. Some seek to improve themselves throughout their life; their goals have a faintly moral cast even though the years also alter their understanding of the goal of self-improvement. Their story tells of a series of different efforts to enhance their person. Others tie their experiences together in a story of improving the world, whether that be in political action, teaching, or some sort of ministry. In some lives, the response to ever new catastrophes and displacements is always the same: rebuilding one's environment, making a new life for oneself, in a new place, under new conditions—always with a characteristic personal style, or certain traditional customs. Some sort of identity arises from the reiteration of certain elements in each new period of one's life, be that the arrangement of one's living space, annual celebrations, characteristic food, or clothes. Others manage to maintain certain principles in the face of political persecution, and to instill those principles in the next generation, and thus a continuity of principles is never breached in their lives and is passed on to others.

These and many other life projects require one to take hold, to be active, to struggle to maintain one's story and to continue it.[2] In spite of all unexpected events, changes one can neither predict nor resist, one refuses to meet those events passively but tries to continue one's project or continue to pursue one's goal. One's efforts assert the importance of one's life, that it matters whether one lives or dies because how one lives matters (Frankl 1974). One can assert the importance of one's life by continuing to adhere to certain principles or by trying to resist the forces that disrupt life: governments hungry for power and territory, businesses determined to grow regardless of the human cost. These are not just stories we tell, but stories we compose as we live them. They are forged in the struggle to maintain some continuity amid the unexpected, unintelligible, and unmanageable events that keep disturbing the flow of life. All such projects give some importance to life; in each there is something that genuinely matters: self-improvement, healing the world, maintaining a certain style in one's life even under very different conditions, never compromising certain principles.

As was true for Ivan Ilych, questions of meaning force themselves on our attention when we suffer. When in pain we want to know whether our suffering can be justified in any way or is simply the imposition of a blind and cruel fate. But Tolstoy's story clearly exhorts us not to wait until pain overwhelms us before striving to make our lives and persons our own, and to weave a life that is to some extent intelligible, where at least some sequences of events can be understood and are sensibly connected to others. Ivan Ilych's story, at the same time, reminds us that we cannot protect ourselves against unforeseen disasters. Human lives are extremely precarious and so is also whatever meaning we may construct for them.

Each effort to give meaning to one's life connects one to groups that share similar values. Political principles are not exclusively one's own; they come out of traditions shared by many persons and organizations. The values one pursues in self-improvement projects are shared by others. One can find them in books or hear them in sermons, or in the exhortations of parents and teachers. The world belongs to all of us; healing it is the project of those of us who perceive its suffering. These efforts often are more successful if they are supported and cheered on by other persons who work alongside us. It is lonely work to be the last defender of freedom in one's town when all others have joined a new totalitarian regime or are hiding fearfully behind locked doors. One is still connected to a long tradition of praising liberty and resisting authoritarian rule in other places. The resistance is less discouraging, however, if one is not alone where one lives, but works together with others who can support one another and cheer each other on. Individuals give meaning to their lives as members of groups, in the name of established traditions, in support of familiar values. The stories they tell about themselves connect their lives to many similar stories or, better yet, engage them in stories lived with others.

For reasons to be clarified later in this chapter and in the next one, not everyone's life sustains such a story. Many live from day to day, like Gregor Samsa, their life significant only because it is a human life. Many attempt to give value to their life by association with a powerful institution. One considers life meaningful because of membership in the party, in the church, or in one's country, because one is working for an important corporation, or is teaching at Harvard. Religious belief in the existence of a supernatural being, all-wise and all-powerful, often is thought to give meaning to life (Klemke 1981). The faithful need not act to assert the value of their life but merely believe and acquiesce in the teachings of a clergy. In all of these associations, one can be quite passive and leave all direction of one's life to the institution under whose wings one finds some spurious safety. One does not choose to identify with a particular sect in the church or throw in one's lot with a specific faction in the party, but leaves that to accident. One does not think about one's country, refusing to entertain any criticism of it. One does not question the usefulness or practices of the corporation that pays one's wages. One obeys blindly the dictates of one's faith and believes whatever absurdity it proclaims.

Religious or political memberships and patriotism are escapes from living a life that has some significance if those memberships are used to evade the labor of making life coherent. Active membership in an organization where one shapes the institution, where one makes choices about the direction it takes, or even abandons it when it takes what one considers a bad turn, will serve to enhance the story of one's life. One may have as a goal to be a good patriot, but that is very different from reciting the Pledge of Allegiance with emotion but cheating on one's taxes, or resisting critical thought about one's country. One may dedicate oneself to a religious existence, but that is different from announcing that one believes in God.[3]

Past, Present, and Future

Life in wartime illustrates the importance of past, present, and future to the formation of self-identity. Peacetime existence, among family and friends, seems very distant and disconnected from life as it is now, constantly imperiled. It is not clear that there is a future; if there is one, it seems impossibly remote. Life is compressed into a limited present. Selves under those conditions appear insubstantial, consisting only of a set of habits, not very securely established because tomorrow's catastrophe may disrupt them. The substance of selves is significantly formed by the connections to a past and a future that extend the present in both directions.

It is often useful to try to revisit the wrong turns taken in the past and to reexamine the patterns of response and behavior that, for an adult, obstruct the possibility of a better life. In being a therapist or availing oneself of one, one acknowledges how much the present is a repetition of the past: Who one was determines who one is today. Anger left over from many years ago, loss, fear, self-doubt, guilt over injuries we did to others, and many other emotions continue to haunt us and distort perceptions of the present. The self that lives in the present is connected to the past in complex ways that are often difficult to bring to light.

But many people, of course, refuse to revisit the past and refuse to reflect about it. If it troubles them, they demand a pill to make them feel better. Learned academics deny the power of the past by writing books demonstrating that psychoanalysis lacks scientific credentials. Others are inveterate storytellers; their past is the source of endless anecdotes that serve to pass the time agreeably, to waste it, while the entertaining stories render the past harmless, amusing but not a power in our present. But one can also make the past all-powerful over the present by presenting oneself as its victim and denying oneself any ability to direct one's life. Alienation is then reinforced by relinquishing any power in the present.

We have some choice as to whether to ignore the past, or make it all-powerful, or try to tame its influence. If we choose to liberate ourselves from past injuries, we move toward being more able, more powerful persons, and some people can do that to an extent. They do improve with age, with hard work and good luck. Here is the kernel of truth in self-realization views of the self. There is no richer, fuller self locked up inside each of us that just needs to be allowed to develop. But under some conditions, some of us manage to rid ourselves of burdens dragged along from the past. To an extent we can free ourselves from those.

Some lives are hobbled not by a past that cannot be overcome but by a present completely discontinuous from the past. Catastrophic changes—the loss of beloved persons, of one's work, one's property or standing in the society, one's country, language, and culture—may well leave one bereft, unable to recognize oneself in the world one inhabits now and incomprehensible to the persons one encounters daily. That is the experience of refugees in time of war; suddenly they find themselves in a different country where they do not speak the language and no one understands them. Accustomed to living on farms, they are now crowded into cities; their children go to new schools, acquire new ways of being, and new ideas that the parents find utterly strange and arouse their suspicions. Who are they in this new world? They defend their identities against the onslaught of a new country, a new language, and a new culture by maintaining what is often a caricature of the culture in the old country. If there are enough of them, they have a radio station that plays the sappy music of long ago. They may maintain some customs of old, teach their children some dances from the old country, and stitch together the costumes worn at dances when they were young. But that does not always suffice to rescue their sense of themselves—an outcome W. G. Sebald (1996) documents elaborately in *The Emigrants*. Sometimes, one's self-identity cannot survive a great catastrophe. A holocaust survivor wrote: "I died in Auschwitz" (Brison 1997).

But one can, of course, minimize those difficulties by choosing to "live in the present," proceeding "one day at a time" and thereby denying that one's relation to the past is one of many dimensions in which one may make some sense of one's life. The immigrant can pretend to be "100 percent American," to have forgotten his native language; he can look down on more recent immigrants as greenhorns. He can talk and act as if his ancestors had been there to welcome the passengers of the *Mayflower*. He can even deny any change in his life by casting away the past, sidestepping the task of linking the present to the past that was so completely different. But his present self is impoverished when the past is denied.

The temptation to forget it is that much greater when the past is burdened with guilt. If we betrayed trust, shirked duty, failed from lack of effort in the crucial moment, or caused others grave injury from inattention or self-indulgence, it is not easy to remember that. It is easier to forget the past, or to rewrite it radically by expunging one's failures. But such evasions leave the self enfeebled. Living a life of one's own may include trying to change in order to repair weaknesses in one's character or to overcome bad habits. If one denies past failings, that becomes impossible. With a past denied, or perhaps drastically revised, one lives in the present; one does not change in significant ways and the self is more shallow. A person, on the other hand, weighed down by guilt, regrets, and self-loathing loses the power to change. The personality becomes congealed; chained forever to past errors, it cannot develop and loses power over a life that, instead, is dominated by the sad past. Whether one ignores guilt or is overwhelmed by it, one succumbs to the precondition of alienation; external forces dominate one's life completely.

If assimilating the past is difficult, so is living in view of the future. Some are defrauded of their present by the hope for a better future. What one has is never good enough. Compared to the promised splendor of the future, one's life and person become insignificant. The future makes constant demands for greater efforts; each day is just one small step on the way to something else, and one's entire life is a chain of way stations to an end one will never reach. Living by one's own life plan may well turn out to be no more than always putting off satisfaction to a future date. One's hope for the future gives meaning to the present, but only if it does not drain the present of its content.

Love

Laf's relation to Martha was full of romance and passion. When they first met he could not stop thinking about her. He proposed marriage in the spring when the lilacs were in bloom. He has since had similar relations and knows that romantic passion often masks ignorance of the person loved. Passion distances lovers rather than bringing them face to face. Passion is also, as Kierkegaard pointed out, often a flight from self. In passion I want to be transported into a different and more exciting world where sensations are more vibrant and where, most important, I am a different person. Passionate love may be a flight from self; a refusal to accept one's life and person as they are; and, at the same time, a refusal to begin with what one has and change it. Liberally laced with fantasy, it is often a refusal to face the world as it is, including its contingency and alienation. Romance cures boredom for the moment but does not change a boring life. It overlays self-hatred as long as I can hide in the fancy garb of the romantic hero. For a while everything is heavy with meaning, my life is one intelligible story overflowing with excitement.

There is little of that passion in Laf's relation to Judi, a relation that began when he was still married. Their love grows during her illness when Laf nurses her and washes her when, after chemotherapy, she has vomited all over herself. None of that encourages romantic passion. Theirs is a different love. It has to do with being present with the other person and not trying to live up to some imaginary ideal of what love should be. Laf understands the change that love has undergone when he finds himself saying that "we"—Judi and he—will fight the cancer. What matters here is not so much the intensity of emotion each partner feels as the commonality of their projects, how ordinary it has become to share, to live life together. He recognizes that he has made a deep commitment, and she to him. Experiencing this other sort of love, Laf has learned something and, in learning it, he has changed. He is more in his life and less inclined to flight into some other, more romantic world. It is easier for him to be in the present, to be terribly open with the other. He is more his own person because he is less eager to escape.

Laf and Judi are "we" and yet Laf is more his own person. The unity that is the essence of love is for many lovers all-encompassing. The separate selves are swallowed up and obliterated in an extraordinary union (Schmitt 1995: ch. 6). But for others, love demands that the lovers unified be clear about their differences. Some lovers engulf each other; others reinforce the independence of each because, strengthened by their unity, they are better able to confront their differences and disagreements. Judi is not convinced that Laf is a writer, but she leaves him be in his effort because she understands how important it is to him. Laf talks to Judi about her previous lives in which, Judi thinks, they had been lovers. Laf does not believe it, and Judi knows that. But remembering her previous existences is important to her; it is the story she tells in order to make sense of her life and he does not want to obstruct that. The love that Judi and Laf discover is austere and shuns self-deception. It is robust enough for them to be able to differ. Only by respecting their different lives and personalities can their love be a celebration of who each person is. The differences are as important as the "we," because the "we" is enriched by the differences.

Such a love that is not threatened by differences strengthens each partner's self-identity. It does not fuse two personalities and promise to make them new but, instead, safeguards each, with their own past and their own future. It enables both to make their lives more their own.

Self as Control

We may be tempted here to think of being oneself, as we often do, as having some control over one's life. Being more in control of his life, we might say, Laf needs fewer romantic evasions to protect himself from reality. But that is wrong. Laf and Judi have no control over her illness or her death. In the short time he can spend with her, he changes, his life changes, but he is hardly in control. He makes some important choices because he chooses to change. For a while it would have been possible to go back to Martha, had he been willing to give up his writing, to go back to teaching English at South High, and be the predictable bourgeois Martha wanted him to be. He recognized that he was no longer able to live that life comfortably and took the risk of moving out, of living with Judi, whose style of loving was very different, who was sick and perhaps would die. Laf half drifted into this different love and different life and half chose it and to that extent lives his own life and is his own person. That he takes risks is saying too much, but he does not avoid them. He is perhaps more active in his life than he once was, but he is certainly not in control of it.

One must beware of claims to be in control of one's life, to run it independently of anyone else, to need no one and be separate from all, for such claims only mask alienation. This is a life in which one is "let alone . . . uninvolved in somebody else's game . . . unobserved . . . " (Kateb 1989:191). The problem posed us by our dual nature—having an animal body and a human mind—is not solved by pretending that one is completely in control, that one is one's own person, the "master of one's ship and the captain of one's soul." Such pretenses conceal our powerlessness, the very limited ability we have to shape our lives. In such protestations of independence and separateness, alienation is not passive but very active—active in creating a gigantic self-deception. Concealed behind this pretense of living one's own life independently of any other person may well be a sad, aimless person whose life makes little more sense than the life of Stoni, Judi's sister, who is forever in pursuit of a new chemical high.

Self-Esteem

As humans, we not only live out the necessities imposed on us by the accidents of our birth, by our place of birth and its conditions, but we also reflect on our lives and choose among alternative lives made possible for us by our bodies and minds, families and environments. In thinking about ourselves, we ask whether we act well, whether we live good lives, whether we are good persons. Self-esteem is an important aspect of our persons, one that yields a sense of our power in the world and how we stand with others, of whether we count for anything and whether we deserve to be loved.

Being willing to change, being willing at times to take risks in order to learn to be a different person, requires that one take oneself seriously. One must value oneself enough to think that learning is important. Martha, safely ensconced behind her desk at the Chancery of the Diocese of Worcester, is only too ready to see herself victimized by Laf. She lacks his courage and his self-esteem. Her orderliness, her worry about the future, her saving money, her compulsive cleaning, betray a self that is fragile. She lacks resilience and thus must build a world for herself that will not challenge her. Laf is more fortunate. A more sturdy sense of himself is a gift, as is his ability to write. Judi is like him in that way. She is strong enough to strike out on her own, away from the troubled lives of the rest of her family. She is strong enough to see her own limitations honestly, as she understands that in her relationship to Laf she is, for the first time, not holding back. Hence they can love without romantic make-believe and learn to be present to one another. Self-esteem is an important condition for resisting alienation.

Self-esteem comes to us only in our lives with others. The sense of self has its origin in the infants' first mutual touching with caretakers and other exchanges of signals that become more complex as children learn to use language. Selves become more clearly felt as they learn to understand particular activities, and their role in them, from the point of view of all the other participants. Learning to play baseball, one learns not only to bat or to catch but to understand one's role from the point of view of the entire complex practice of playing baseball. One can't play the game without understanding the rules, who the other players are, what they do, and how one's own role looks from their perspective. And just as with all other things that one learns, one must always understand the entire practice and how what one does at this moment fits into it. George Herbert Mead (1934:154–155) called this "taking the attitude of the generalized other."

To be a self, one must be able to see oneself from the point of view of the entire group that participates in a particular activity. The self comes to be seen from the inside only as one also learns to see it from the outside.

From others one learns not only to understand what one is doing but also to judge whether one does it well. As a child one acquires a sense of what it is good to do and what not. One must "introject" parental authority, Freud said. Children learn, as they grow up, to manage their own behavior without adult supervision. After a while you do not need to remind them to put on hats and gloves when it is cold out, or to tie their shoelaces; they will do that on their own. They will change their clothes and clean up their rooms without being told by anyone to do so. The parental voice has been internalized. That voice, in Freud's story, is mostly negative: It threatens, it chastises. But, in fact, the parental voice we make our own also praises and tells us not only that we are loved but also, sometimes, that we do well, that our life has promise, that happiness may be in store for us. Making this voice their own, children learn to judge themselves and try to maintain their self-esteem. They take upon themselves tasks for which, before, they needed reminders. They also learn to take pleasure in what they do and in doing it well. One's sense of oneself reflects the observations and judgments of many other persons.

The eminent psychologist Heinz Kohut has pointed out that the nascent self, as it develops, also requires someone to respond to its needs. An infant acquires a sense of power in the world when she gets what she demands. Here is the beginning of a sense of efficacy that is so essential to self-esteem: the sense that if one wants something, one can sometimes make it happen. The child begins to learn that she can express her needs and get someone to listen and that she can, thereby, satisfy her desires. She learns that she can be effective in the world by inducing others to act as she wants them to act (Kohut 1977). The confidence needed in order to be selves in a social world is not just a feeling ("feeling good about oneself"); it is knowing oneself to be effective in the world. Self-confidence must be anchored in real capacities. But these capacities depend, partly, on others. Whether Laf will turn out to be a writer depends on whether he will find publishers and readers receptive to his writing. His confidence that he will find himself to be a writer if only he perseveres includes faith not only in his own talent but also in the existence of editors and readers ready to read his stories with care and an open mind. Self-confidence includes a sense of not being all alone, of not being cast out into a merciless world. Self-confidence is, in part, trust in the goodwill of others.

In order to be oneself in this sense of knowing that one can manage in the world, one needs not only to see others but to be seen by them, as who one is. One must receive praise and blame, love and rejection. To be oneself and confident in that self, one needs recognition from others. The infant needs parents to respond to her cries; Laf needs sympathetic readers. As Judi suffers through her illness, she needs Laf to be there patiently and to remember that in this sick, emaciated, wracked body is a beloved human being. Only when we are recognized by others in the right ways can we develop the free confidence to take up space in the world, to let the world know who we are, what we need and want, and to give as generously as we receive. Only in relation to others can we be a self—the sort of self that, for instance, forms life plans, adopts its own values, endorses its desires, or tells stories that make sense of our life. What is more, it is only in relation to concrete other persons that we develop a sense of ourselves.

Such self-confidence must, of course, be tentative if it is not to lose sight of the overwhelming contingency of human life. A brash confidence in one's own power to carry out a carefully chosen life project misrepresents the world in which one lives and translates the pursuit of one's goal into a quixotic fantasy exploit. Blind confidence in oneself, the belief that one can do anything one sets one's mind to, perpetuates alienation by obliterating the overwhelming power of contingency in human life and the limits imposed on humans' efforts to make sense of their lives. The feel-good self-confidence of readers of self-help books or members of religious or psychological cults tries to abbreviate the extended process of building self-confidence. Ignoring the need for patient strengthening of one's capacities, acknowledging failures, and trying to learn to do better, alienation is exacerbated by pretending that a few simple mantras, repeated endlessly, will overcome the fundamental ambiguities of human life. What is needed are not good feelings so much as confident action, being at home in the world, as shown by the ease in which one moves around in it. Feigned self-confidence is another cover for alienation.

Recognition Is Central to Being Oneself

What is this recognition that is so essential to being a self? In recent years, political philosophers have insisted that groups are entitled to have their cultural specificities recognized. This claim is used, for instance, to bolster the right of French-speaking Canadians to take measures to preserve their language and customs in largely English-speaking and Anglo-Saxon Canada. Members of different cultural groups are entitled to recognition of what is unique about their cultures because all citizens are entitled to respect. Since the culture to which they belong constitutes, in part, who they are, respect for each citizen includes treasuring the language of each, as well as the customs of ethnic, national, racial communities (Taylor 1992:36ff.).

This demand for the recognition of different groups arises from a heightened awareness of the damage done where such recognition has been withheld. African-Americans and other persons of color have spoken out about the harms inflicted by a racism that assumed that, because they were not white, they did not deserve the same respect as whites. African-Americans in the United States

> were born into a society which spelled out with brutal clarity, and in as many ways as possible, that . . . [they] . . . were worthless human being[s]. . . . The details and symbols of . . . [their] . . . life were deliberately constructed to make . . . [whites] . . . believe what they said about . . . [them]. (Baldwin 1963:7–8)

If I talk to, work for, spend time with, study with, teach, or repair the car of someone who regards me as, of course, stupid because of the color of my skin, or because I speak English with an accent, my cleverness and skills cannot develop. What I say to that person may come out of my mouth intelligent but is heard as gibberish. He therefore reacts angrily, or at best patronizingly, closing off the space in which I can be intelligent. Intelligence is not private; it must be exercised, and that exercise requires that I be able to talk and *be heard* as the intelligent person I am. In a society where I am thought to be dull, opportunities for being intelligent are foreclosed because I will not be allowed in schools where my intelligence can flourish. The recognition one needs to discover that one is intelligent is withheld from the victims of prejudice, and thus they cannot even discover that they are, in fact, talented.

Recognition opens up that space between persons in which we can be strong, resourceful, insightful, patient. The targets of racial, gender, and other prejudices do not receive that recognition from the dominant group and accordingly are not allowed the opening to develop firm selves in relation to the more powerful. In order to be able to grow into strong human beings, they must find safe spaces of their own, away from the detraction by dominant groups.

Consider, for the moment, different uses of the word *recognition:* "I recognize the delegate from Outer Mongolia," "I recognized his voice immediately," "We give you this plaque in recognition of fifty years of faithful service." Recognition may consist of registering someone's presence, identifying someone, or acknowledging a person's merit.

There are correspondingly different ways to fail to get recognition. One's existence may be unacknowledged and that makes one literally invisible. We do this to servants, persons whose jobs are regarded as menial, and, often, to children. In *The Feminine Mystique,* Betty Friedan (1964) pointed to the "problem that has no name"—the dissatisfaction of many suburban housewives with the life they found themselves leading. But as long as no one was willing to recognize that such a life is not for everyone, the problem did not exist. It could not be articulated; the categories of acceptable complaints did not encompass the dissatisfaction with suburban motherhood and homemaking. Problems unrecognized cannot be diagnosed. The reality of women's lives in certain suburban settings remained hidden. Failure to recognize someone often also takes the form of misidentifying him, or what he does. One misunderstands, responds in inappropriate ways to the other. Often that takes the form of stereotyping. Many adults stereotype children, treating each like all the others, instead of as individuals as different from one another as adults are. Failure to be recognized may, in addition, mean that one's presence is acknowledged, one is correctly identified, but that one's person is denigrated—the frequent experience of men and women of color, of women in general, of children and the old. Here one's presence is acknowledged but one's valuable qualities, hidden behind the stereotype, are not recognized.

Recognition is not only intellectual, a matter of seeing, liking, taking seriously the other. Recognition is also enacted. To recognize another person, in the sense that counts here, is to let oneself be affected by the other. Parents who respond to the infant's cry allow the child to affect them and shape their behavior. Recognition is reading another's work, offering help when there seems a need, or asking for help from others who appear willing to offer assistance. Recognition involves listening with care and speaking one's own mind to show oneself for who one is. Recognition involves acknowledging another's skills and talents and promoting them, if one can. Recognition requires action and reaction.

Responding to the infant's cry, reading a friend's poetry, listening, helping, telling stories about oneself are ways of completing another's act (Noddings 1984). The person who writes becomes a writer when her work is read; the child's existence is confirmed by the response of his parents. Actions are public and must be recognized and acknowledged for what they are. What is done in private remains ambiguous. I may habitually steal things but remain undetected. Am I a thief? I tell myself that I am really fortunate to find all sorts of useful things, which I squirrel away where no one can see them. But I do not think of myself as a thief and do not become one until I am discovered and publicly branded as one. If a man sports women's underwear strictly in private, it is not clear what he is doing. Perhaps he is to trying to titillate himself, just fooling around, or seeing what it feels like; but he might also be fantasizing about what it means to be a woman. To be an unmistakable cross-dresser he needs to show himself in public dressed as a woman. But if you parade down the street in clothes of the opposite sex once or twice, are you a transvestite, or someone who is just beginning to try out this other life, or someone who is not really serious about it and is mocking the lives of gender changers? Are you mocking women or yourself? To be a transvestite you must be accepted as one by others who have seen you as serious in your changes of gender identity. A red rubber nose and white face paint don't make you a circus clown; neither does donning the clown's costume to amuse three-year-olds at a birthday party. There is a world of circus clowns, and in order to be one of them you need to belong to this world. One's acts must be recognized for what they are; they must be completed by others. Lacking recognition they remain unclear, open to different interpretations, or perhaps quite meaningless. So, far from being independent, separate from others, one must, in order to be oneself, be a recognized member of a group, or of many groups, to be the different persons that one is. Recognition is a precondition of personal identity and of self-knowledge.

Recognition Is, At Its Best, Mutual

It matters a great deal where we get recognition and from whom. A German movie of the silent film era, *Der letzte Mann*,[4] depicts the doorman in a fancy hotel. He is treated with deference when he returns at night to the tenement where he lives still wearing his resplendent uniform. But then he loses his job and with it his eminent position in the neighborhood, for he had been respected for his uniform, not for his person. To be sure, his impressive appearance depended in part on his own efforts. He had to bear himself with dignity, address his superiors with deference without being subservient, and speak firmly but kindly to the shoe shine boys and messengers. But once the job is gone, so is his uniform and the opportunity to wear it with dignity. What is left is an utterly private person, known to no one for no one has managed to see him as a person in his own right. Since all the recognition he received was riveted to the uniform, once that was gone he disintegrated.

The porter, living in a shabby working-class tenement, can receive more respect from his neighbors than they show for one another. For his uniform he can be singled out as a more important person than anyone else, and it is difficult to resist the temptation to invite such respect. But, once deprived of the uniform, he pays the price of complete anonymity and loss of identity for that recognition. It is difficult to resist the temptation of accepting the special treatment one can receive for being a doctor, a professor, a television personage, an actor or athlete, for being a rich man in a small town. But, as in the case of the porter, such veneration of one's public persona comes at a price. Recognition of this sort does not nurture the self. It does not support one in developing a firmer identity, or in strengthening those aspects of oneself that one considers more important and closer to the core of one's existence.

Recognition that is addressed to my person, rather than to my public role—to my splendid uniform, as it were—completes my actions. Such completions may create controversy. You take my joke as an insult, or feel criticized by what I said in order to praise you. Actions are, after all, subject to varying interpretations and those may need to be negotiated. But not all completions of my actions, not all recognitions, are negotiable. In situations of unequal power, between citizen and policeman, between student and teacher, often between parent and child, the interpretation given by the powerful person sticks and no negotiation is possible. Recognition that fortifies the self often needs to be scrutinized by both the actor and the person who completes the action. It is most fruitful where differences in power do not foreclose needed conversations.

The admiration of persons I do not know cannot be nearly as significant to me as the measured praise from those whose work, or character, or life I respect and take as a model for mine. Strangers who make much of me may turn out to have terrible judgment; being admired by them is a severe condemnation. Recognition that fortifies selves must be mutual. It must be bestowed by those whom I respect, with whom I work productively, and whose company enriches my days. It is most readily available where work is shared and each makes a very specific contribution to a joint project. There a number of persons form a "we," as Judi and Laf do, it is clear from the contribution each makes who everyone is. Such common spaces are not limited to the shared lives of lovers. In schools, in car pools, in neighborhood associations, in clubs, the members share a project, however limited in scope it may be; within those limits, different persons make their contribution. The functioning of the group requires that the contributions of each be known so that everyone knows who is driving the kids to school on Wednesday morning, or who will buy the food for the Saturday-night party at the American Legion Hall. Identities are fortified by sharing work with others for a common purpose. Anchored in the work of groups, identities are that much firmer than those dependent on being recognized by one other person. Recognition by the members of the group is refracted by the many different personalities and outlooks of the members that thereby enrich the person I am.

Recognition is sometimes, but not always, respectful or even affectionate. Some recognize us admiringly; others regard us as enemies, as threats to their well-being and way of life. Minnie Bruce Pratt describes how she grew up as the daughter of a prominent upper-class white Southern family. She married the suitable son of a similar Southern family and the couple had children. Then she fell in love with another woman and came out as a lesbian. A nasty divorce ensued; her children were taken away from her. She settled down with her Jewish lover in a black neighborhood in Washington, DC. She maintains her relationship with her family; they know her but they no longer acknowledge her with pride. Perhaps still with love, but now in pain, they reject the life she has chosen and the values she embodies and promotes in her writing. They recognize her as a threat to their way of life and values (Pratt 1984). One may recognize a person admiringly; but one recognizes others as opponents, albeit worthy ones. As Nietzsche insists, having enemies provides an important form of recognition. "You may only have enemies whom you can hate, not enemies you despise. You must be proud of your enemy: the successes of your enemy are your successes too" (Nietzsche 1954:158). One respects a worthy enemy. This respect helps to define who each person is as well as to bolster their respect for themselves.

In mutual relations of recognition I may be changed. I see others live in ways that seem admirable to me and I try to emulate them. In order to cement a relationship, I see that I need to change in certain ways; I need to moderate my anger, or be less critical, or be more articulate about what I value in the other. I may need to take responsibility for things that I left for the other to do, or make room for the other to take on work that traditionally has been mine in the relationship. Martha always complained that Laf did not do any housework. With Judy ill, Laf does it all. More important, Judi keeps telling Laf that he is an angry person and he, because he does not yell and have noisy tantrums, does not believe her. But as they grow closer together and trust each other more, he hears what she says and though he does not know how to change himself—he wonders whether she wants him to scream at her—it is clear that he has at that moment begun to change. He is taking her seriously because he loves her; he is trying to please her. But he is listening because he thinks that maybe she is right. Not only does he trust her judgment but perhaps he has an inkling that, yes, he harbors a good deal of anger. If he is changing, it is always as Laf, the wisecracking, storytelling writer, the man capable of enormous patience and gentleness in caring for someone he loves. The changes Laf will make in close relations are modifications of the person he is.

Recognition, Conformism, and Alienation

Judi's family loves small appliances, any new gadget that does what you had not known needed to be done. For the alienated, whose lives are without shape, boredom is an ever-present threat and any new thing, any new toy, can dispel boredom for a while. The ever-accelerating changes of popular culture are designed to keep boredom at bay, to divert and distract. Producers of entertainments dream up ever-new absurdities to titillate, shock, and provide topics of conversation that stay far enough away from the speaker's life not to cause any embarrassment or anxiety. Mass entertainment has become a gigantic business because so many persons' lives are too incomprehensible and too random to give them any sort of shape.

The alienated do not gain their self-esteem from mutual recognition. No one in their world has a clear self to be recognized. Self-esteem comes instead from appearing acceptable, being liked, not being embarrassingly different. If you have no sense of what sort of person you are, or what is a good life for you, and if you spend your days working and trying to have fun in any way possible, then you cannot gain recognition for being a very specific person. Because life just flows along, your person is a jumble of traits, activities, and thoughts that form no whole and make little sense. Persons seeking to shape some sort of identity of their own will not seek your company. You must therefore look for recognition from others who are also just taking their life as it comes. You try to get along, to be respected, liked for not being different, for fitting in, being familiar. In this condition, one does not want to be liked by others whose lives, although perhaps different, one respects. One wants, instead, to be up to date, wear what the fashion magazines tout, drive the latest car, and have all the gadgets imaginable. This too is a search for a kind of recognition. But now one does not want recognition for being a writer, or a decent person, or a gentle lover. One wants recognition for meeting standards of appearance, of "life-style," of opinions and practices that are set by some impersonal public power, which, in our day, primarily comprises the mass media and the industries that control them. Fashions in clothes are most familiar, but there are fashions in furnishing your house, raising your children, and spending your leisure time. There are, similarly, fashions in the arts, in literature, in philosophy and the social sciences. Conformism remains the only choice. Conformity is not the cause of alienation, as Rousseau and Tolstoy thought, but its symptom. The pervasive mass culture purveys alienation.

Who's to Blame? Alienation and Luck

It is tempting to blame the alienated for their condition. Rousseau considered alienation to be due to the failures of individuals who choose to be conformist and slaves to public opinion. And Tolstoy thought that Ivan Ilych chose the path of conformism when, as a boy, he succumbed to peer pressure to do something that he himself regarded as rather "horrid." Tolstoy had little sympathy for the dying Ivan Ilych. But Ivan followed in the footsteps of his father and was probably a more responsible and competent bureaucrat than any of his brothers. All his friends lived as he did, concerned only about how they appeared to others and wanting, above all, not to be different, but not caring whether they lived their life well. As Tolstoy tells the story, Ivan Ilych had never learned that one could live differently. It is then not surprising that his life should have turned out as it did. One does not choose a way of life that one has never seen, that is totally unknown, or, even if known, has always been presented as reprehensible. Growing up in a society where everyone is a careerist, where gossip about the smallest departures from convention is the daily staple of conversation, one would not think of living differently. Nor is choosing to live a different life enough; one must know how to do that. Then Ivan tries once, in decorating his new house, to strike out for himself and to do something different, the result is a sad failure because he has never cultivated his taste. He has always liked what everyone else liked, and accordingly his new house is quite conventional and uninteresting. Living a life of one's own needs to be learned and not everyone is given the opportunity to learn it.

Writers about alienation tend to look down on the alienated, but without reason. They forget that we are not born knowing how to make our lives our own and to put them in some semblance of order. That is something we learn gradually and by fits and starts. Until she met Laf, Judi had had relationships with married men and she understood very well the attraction of that: The relationships were always limited. She did not have to share her house with another person, nor her life. Sharing involves surrendering some control to the other; not sharing allowed her to retain complete control over herself. With Laf, Judi learns to share. They both learn that there is a love that allows the partners to be different and that these differences need not be concealed. At the same time, both discover that they can share a life with someone else and that each can try to protect the other a little bit. In the course of these lessons, each learns to be more independent; they acquire a new hold on their own self-identities.

None of this is learned from books. If self-help books worked, there would not be so many of them. But having found all the previous ones useless, we want more advice, hoping always that someone will be able to tell us how to live our lives right. But no one can just tell us how to do that, although with luck, we sometimes find another to help us learn the needed lessons. We learn what we need to know by doing. Laf and Judi find themselves, mostly by accident, in a situation where they learn how to live with another person differently from what they had managed before. They did not set out to learn these lessons; they did not even know that the lessons were there to be learned. It was sheer good luck that they found themselves in a situation where they could change a little bit. They were very fortunate.

If we are lucky to find ourselves in the right situation, we may learn to overcome the precondition of alienation to some extent. But some environments provide many more opportunities than others for learning that. Alienation has social roots. Some societies systematically starve their members of the opportunities to learn how to live lives of their own. I will discuss some of these social conditions inhibiting personal integration in the next chapter.

What, Then, Is Alienation?

We have traveled a long way from the idea of alienation as the failure to coincide with one's self, or of developing the self hidden inside of us all along, or of being autonomous by leading a life according to our own life plan. We have seen, on the one hand, that human lives are animal lives, embodied, ruled by natural necessity and blind accident, and, on the other hand, that we are thinking beings. Often we reflect before we act or reconsider afterward and judge our actions good or bad. We want to live good lives that makes sense. It matters to us what sorts of persons we are. We try to understand and, sometimes, to change ourselves.

This duality of our nature is the precondition of alienation. We may ignore our ability to think about and, to a limited extent, affect our existence, living from day to day, and allowing accident and circumstances, including demands that others make on us, to determine our life history. This is alienation: when life makes little sense because no one expects it to have meaning or when efforts to find meaning in it fail. One day follows another, often boring and repetitive, sometimes utterly catastrophic, but always incomprehensible and not under anyone's control at all. That leaves many alienated in a second sense, of *feeling* depressed, aimless, without any power, out of place, without a home or a proper place in the world.

The tension between our animal nature and our ability to think about ourselves is the essence of our humanity and the precondition of alienation. How we respond to this tension is to some extent up to us. We can submit to the precondition of alienation or strive for a partial understanding of our lives and our persons. These efforts to give some shape to our lives are not reserved for special, dramatic junctures in our life histories; they occur daily. Everyday choices reinforce alienation or increase, if only incrementally, our ability to understand and direct our existence. In this chapter we have examined some of the issues in human lives that, depending on how we address them, either increase alienation or diminish it a bit. In each area of our lives a series of decisions challenge us to confront alienation and to make our lives our own.

Alienated lives lack intelligibility. No human life is completely transparent; accident rules human existence and shapes it for reasons that one cannot understand. But to varying extents some persons manage to give some coherence to their lives in many different ways. Some lives are animated by a central project, others by the maintenance of certain principles, be they moral or political. A pervasive style connects the different episodes in still other lives. Some unfold as stories that make sense; past, present, and future are connected in ways that form a continuous whole. Those who have a clear identity live a life that is, to an extent, comprehensible because each portion of such a life expresses that identity. A firm identity or definite self requires that one affirm oneself; one requires self-esteem in order to lead a life that is, to an extent, one's own and manifests who one is. Self-esteem, in turn, accrues from the recognition one gains from others, whom one recognizes in turn. Acknowledged for the unique person one is, one can be a person in one's own right. Ultimately the intelligibility of human lives is grounded in relations to other members of groups.

Every human life is different and thus alienation takes different forms for each. Laf is quite clear about the way his worklife should go. In matters of love he is less certain. Martha, from the outset a more timid person, has to take a very different road to make some sense of her life. Because each life is different and each person has different capacities, each confronts the challenge to give meaning to life in different situations. Work is a frequent source of alienation, but not for everyone. Love is a consolation for some, and for others the poverty of their life is most obvious in their close relations to others. The general formulae we use to speak of alienation must never conceal the fact that each struggles with the precondition of alienation in unique ways.

What sort of choices we make, how difficult it is for us to be more active and more powerful in our lives, depends on the external conditions that our society provides for us. There are many forces that impair our ability to understand ourselves and to function actively and purposefully in our lives. In the next chapter we will consider some of the social forces in our society that enhance alienation.

Notes

1. And the question of what a satisfactory account of one's different selves and different lives is only opens another very large conversation.

2. We are not guaranteed a meaningful life merely by virtue of being active. Ivan Ilych was actively pursuing the good opinion of others. That left him, as he discovered, with a life that lacked significance. In order to make life meaningful, activity must be in one's own behalf, in order, as we saw in the preceding section, to make one's life one's own.

3. The claim made so often by ministers and other interested parties that life has meaning only if one believes in God is deceptive marketing. Like most advertising it appeals to our laziness and passivity, promising us instant meaning without effort. That is a fraud reflecting badly on the religions that perpetrate it.

4. *Der letzte Mann* (also known, in the United States, as *The Last Man* or *The Last Laugh*) (1924), German, B&W. Directed by F. T. Murnau. Cast: Emil Jannings, Mady Delschaft, Max Hiller, and Emilie Kurz (retrieved from the World Wide Web, November 30, 2001, at http://www.silentera.com/PSFL/data/L/LetzteMann1924.html).

4

THE SOCIAL ROOTS OF ALIENATION

Are humans everywhere beset by alienation, or only in specific social systems? Both sides to the extended controversy about this question have captured an important part of the truth. Alienation can exist because we have bodies burdened by necessity and minds that desire freedom. This duality of human nature makes it possible for humans to be alienated but does not give rise to alienation in all cultures. It receives different interpretations in different times and places. Not alienation itself, but its precondition, is rooted in human nature. It grows into alienation in some social worlds.

The European Middle Ages were well acquainted with the experience of what we call alienation, but they had a different name for it. They called it "acedia," spiritual lassitude, and meant by that the unwillingness to accept spiritual discipline because it had come to seem pointless. Acedia was a kind of despair. In a religious age requiring stern religious practice, despair was a hindrance to religious devotion and that is how despair was understood (Wenzel 1967). Our conception of the good life, such as the development of individuality, of being a person in one's own right, of living a life of one's own, of being in some ways independent and autonomous, made little sense in the medieval world because persons did not matter for their own sake but only as servants of God. Many persons today believe that each individual must be free to choose his or her own stance with respect to religion. The individual's choices take precedence over the demands of the divine—a blasphemous view in the eyes of medieval Christianity. We believe that being one's own person and living one's own life are important tasks, which include ascertaining one's attitude toward religion and acting on those decisions. In a world of religious devotion, the despair occasioned by the condition of alienation was perceived as an interruption of the required spiritual exercises. Only in the modern world, where persons count as individuals, does the duality of human lives become the origin of alienation, as the failure to be oneself, because it interferes, not with religious devotion, but with efforts to make sense of one's life or to be one's own person.

Social systems matter to alienation in another way. Unless they have already given up, and live aimlessly from day to day, or claim to have overcome alienation because they live according to their own life plan, persons struggle against the precondition of alienation and try to make sense of life in spite of it. But no one is born knowing how to do that. One learns it gradually if one finds opportunities for acquiring the requisite skills and understanding. One's environment can promote or obstruct that effort. Extreme poverty compels one to scrabble for food and shelter and detracts from any other effort to shape one's life; it makes impossible even a minimal emancipation of oneself from harsh economic necessity. Poverty seriously limits choices, as do different group oppressions. They damage self-esteem and obstruct efforts to be one's own person. This chapter will examine obstacles to learning how to live one's own life that are created by social conditions.

Living one's own life, making sense of it, being oneself, is not a project one accomplishes once and for all. In many different situations throughout one's life, events call its meaning into question; the self is thrown into confusion by external forces. As one reaches adulthood, one must create a worklife of one's own, one must manage the different personalities that dwell in one's body, in order to present oneself to the world and to oneself as a reasonable person. The past must be assimilated if it was painful; one must try to establish continuing ties to a past that is quite different from the present. Establishing continuity is a challenge for some; others must introduce variety into a life dreary in its daily sameness. The future must animate the present with hope without devaluing what we have today. Without hope the present is gray and feeble. If all we live on is hope, the present is rendered worthless. Life is constantly moved along by unforeseen events, of which death is only one of the more spectacular ones. Making sense of one's life means maintaining a coherent narrative of one's life without making up fantastic stories. Being oneself requires that one solidify identity and bolster self-esteem by receiving and giving recognition. In many lives, recognition is gained by loving and being loved, by being steadfast as a lover and friend. But self-esteem also becomes firmer when one shows courage and stoicism in great crises, when one learns to be resilient amidst the setbacks of one's existence.

Not everyone can do all of those things. Since each person is different from the others, the challenges to selfhood are different for each. Each must learn how to make sense of his or her life, as it unfolds, by acquiring the skills needed to meet the tasks set by the precondition of alienation. In some social settings it is more difficult to acquire the necessary skills than in others. Our society, in spite of extolling individuality and independence, makes it very difficult to lead lives of our own. The following sections will describe how our society prevents us from acquiring the skills needed for constructing a solid self.[1]

Once again we will take a novelist as our guide in exploring the ways in which our society promotes alienation.

Emma Bovary: Life in the Market Society

Emma Bovary's is a story of dreams and longing, adulterous love, and, finally, suicide (Flaubert 1989). Her mother having died a few years before, she keeps house for her father on his prosperous farm. There are wagons and carts and several ploughs stored in a barn, large and well maintained, as are the sheepfold and other outbuildings. On the great manure pile in the farmyard, five or six peacocks, a luxury on Normandy farms, are rooting for food among the ducks and the turkeys. Emma cooks for her father and the farmhands in an enormous open fireplace. She supervises the servants doing the washing, hanging the white sheets flapping in the spring sunshine. Many women would have been content with this life and would have welcomed marriage to a farmer, and children, and years of hard work until old age brought rest and death. But Emma wants more. The rustic life is not for her. She is not only very good-looking but also bright, energetic, and, having gone to convent school, accomplished in drawing and playing the piano. She is, at times, an avid reader. Unlike many others, content to take life as it comes, doing the work closest at hand, Emma is a dreamer.[2] She wants to make something of her life more powerful than life on the farm offers her. When Charles Bovary, a country doctor who comes to set her father's broken leg, falls in love with her, she marries him and knows, a few days afterward, that she has made a mistake.

Emma wants her life to have meaning; she wants it to be important. For her that means that it should be filled with passion, intense happiness, and rapture. Boredom is the fierce enemy. As the doctor's wife in a small country town, her existence is too calm, too monotonous for her to feel that she matters. For a while she tries to be a good wife to Charles, and to manage the house well. She also tries to infuse some romance into their relationship. But Charles, a kind-hearted man who loves her deeply, is not very bright, his conversation is commonplace, and he is a stranger to romance. He cannot share Emma's dreams. They are not suited to each other. When they are invited to a ball at a nearby country estate, Emma sees the splendid life of the very wealthy at firsthand. Returning to their modest house afterward, she falls into a deep depression.

Charles decides that she needs a change of scene. Reluctantly he decides to leave Tostes, where he has been building up a good practice, to move to a different country town, depressingly like Tostes, in order to give Emma a change of scenery. There Emma continues her search for a life that means more than her dull routine, for a kindred soul, who has some inkling of what she longs for, for someone who will recognize her for who she is and break her isolation. Most of all, she is looking for passion, the transports that make the world look new every day, that garbs in splendor the shabby existences of the rural bourgeois.

When they arrive in their new home, in Yonville, she meets Leon, a law student clerking for the local notary, and here her dream promises to be fulfilled. Leon too is bored by country life. They talk about the city, about Paris and the splendid life everyone leads there, the parties, the masked balls, and the duels in the Bois. They fall in love, they take chaste walks and have soulful conversations; but Leon is too young and timid for adultery, and Emma is not yet ready for it. Their love remains platonic. Then Leon leaves; he actually gets to live in Paris in order to complete his legal studies. Rodolphe, a wealthy bachelor who lives near Yonville, decides to seduce Emma on the sunny Sunday of the annual agricultural fair. Thile visiting dignitaries orate tediously about patriotism, civilization, and progress downstairs in the square, he and Emma are sitting at the town hall window, overlooking the festivities, and Rodolphe speaks passionately about his love for her. For some months, their torrid affair is just what she has been hoping for; but passion of such intensity cannot be sustained. Gradually, they settle into the routine of an old married couple. Then Emma wants Rodolphe to carry her away to some dreamy, foreign land, he leaves her. She almost dies of grief.

But she recovers. When Leon returns from Paris, to be a law clerk in Rouen, the nearby provincial capital, they have a sultry love affair. But once again, their ardor is not sustainable. The relationship ends because Emma is looking for a passion that cannot last and because Leon, in spite of all his brave talk about living arduously in defiance of convention, wants nothing more than to settle into the respectability of being a small-town lawyer.

Emma has all along been seduced into financial extravagances by the local haberdasher and loan shark, L'Heureux. Now, betrayed once more, she discovers that she owes a large debt without any possibility of paying it back. The contents of her house are about to be sold at public auction while she, frantically, appeals to her former lovers, to Rodolphe, to Leon, for financial assistance. Both refuse. Distraught, feeling totally abandoned by everyone, she swallows a handful of arsenic and dies miserably. Charles abandons his practice, becomes a recluse, and dies not too long after Emma.

Many readers of Flaubert's *Madame Bovary* refuse Emma their sympathy. She is a silly woman who has read too many romantic novels—so thought Henry James, perhaps because Emma is not as full of high-minded conversation, or as rich, as James's Isabel Archer (Flaubert 1989). Flaubert encourages that interpretation when he talks about the otherworldly atmosphere in Emma's convent school—a mixture of transcendent religion and the trashy romantic novels the girls read surreptitiously. But her novel reading does not explain the tragedy of her life. That story is much more complex and more interesting.

Her misfortunes begin with being born who she is, strong and gifted, on a farm in Normandy in the middle of the nineteenth century. From the very beginning, necessity plays a powerful role. Emma is hemmed in on all sides by circumstances not under her control. Genetic accidents made her brighter and more capable than most of the people around her. They also made her a woman. She keeps telling the men she loves that, unlike them, she cannot do anything with her life. For her, no profession is open; she cannot go away to school and develop her intellectual powers. She cannot travel, have adventures, and fight duels. She cannot make money or become famous by doing extraordinary deeds. In spite of her significant abilities, she is cooped up in the house, limited to supervising the servants. Her generous imagination is wasted in engaging in wild adulterous affairs with men who do not love her.

At the same time, she wants to make something of her life. She is not ready to acquiesce in what accident has brought her; she is not willing to accept her life as it has begun and make do with that. She accepts the challenge presented by the precondition of alienation. But conditions are very unfavorable for making her life hang together, making sense of it, and making it her own. The world in which she lives does not present her with models to emulate or persons who are living their life as if it was theirs and all of a piece. Instead she is surrounded by people who, if they are not content with everything, either are busy getting ahead or are hopeless romantics dreaming of a different life in a faraway place. Her society throws up a series of obstacles to making a life for herself. Alienation is encouraged by her society and, in very similar ways, by ours.

Great strength of character and much more self-love than Emma could muster would have been needed to resist the mind-numbing boredom of bourgeois life in the small towns where her husband practiced medicine. Emma needed love; she needed the affirmation that strong passion brings.

With that she might have been able to keep drawing, to keep playing the piano, to keep reading, in order to have some sort of life her own. But she lived in a society where women counted for little and were not entitled to lives that mattered, where money and appearances were valued more than substantial merit. Her vitality found no constructive outlet; she was crushed by the emptiness of her life, as was everybody else. Lacking confidence in her own rightness, unconvinced that she mattered and that her actions were important, she gave all that up and fled into buying luxury goods to assuage her grief over her lost life. Her self-love was corroded by the pursuit of money, appearances, and deceptions. Her tragedy is emblematic of the sterility of bourgeois society.

The Importance of Money

Calvin Coolidge, the New England small-town lawyer who became president of the United States, is remembered for saying that "America's business is business" and that "civilization and profit go hand in hand." Coolidge would have been quite at home in the mid–nineteenth-century small towns in Normandy where money was on everyone's mind and everyone sought to get more. Charles Bovary's father married his mother for her money. Charles himself, fresh from his medical training, was married off in his early twenties to a fortyish widow, scrawny, with pimples and a bad temper, because she was reputed to own some property. After her death, he marries Emma. The guests at Emma's wedding, when they were not playing tricks on each other, were talking business, and business was the topic of conversation at the public dinner at the end of the agricultural fair in Yonville where Emma was living a year or two later. Emma's father did not like farming because, he said, it never yet made anyone a millionaire. For him, too, what mattered in life was getting rich. In Yonville, L'Heureux is constantly conniving to sell Emma things she cannot afford and lending her money to do so. He and the notary are involved in shady speculations with mortgages.

Emma is not immune to this commercial spirit. "She wanted," writes Flaubert, "to get some personal profit out of things" (p. 72). She too would have liked to have more money. When first pregnant, she wanted to buy expensive things for the baby, but not being able to afford them, she refuses to have anything more to do with the preparations for the birth. Having a child was an opportunity for buying pretty things and when that proved impossible, she lost interest. She is moved, Flaubert says, "by the lusts of the flesh and the longing for money" (p. 219). She pines for the wealthy life she observes at the country estate where she attends a ball; she is enchanted with the luxurious objects in Rodolphe's house. When she is depressed, she buys expensive trinkets to soothe her suffering. Emma is steeped in the materialism of her world. "She confused . . . The sensualities of luxury with the delights of the heart" (p. 119). She mistook for the joys of deep love, slowly nurtured over time, the romantic settings in faraway countries, the wealth thrown away on great houses, on balls, on comfortable coaches and great traveling cloaks.

The error is typical of the consumer society. There money is at the center, so are the things that money can buy. Much confusion is spread by the ubiquity of commodities in the market society. Emma's belief that love requires the properly romantic setting is one such error. The relationship between two persons, which is the essence of love, must grow, be nurtured and worked on. Money has little to contribute here. The material setting of that relationship, the romantic places, the extravagantly expensive wedding, the new home furnishings and clothes tend, in a world where money is all important, to overwhelm the demands of building a relationship. Great life events like pregnancy and childbirth are transformed into commercial occasions to make more purchases, concealing the opportunities for building selves and constructing meaning. The birth of a child challenges the parents to become a father or a mother in keeping with who they are already, or to transform those selves to accommodate parenting. But in the orgy of purchases and of receiving gifts for mother and baby, the occasions for strengthening the self are pushed into the background and tend to get overlooked.

In the World of Money, Appearances Are All That Matter

The belief that money makes a good life is widely shared in Emma's world, as it is in ours, even though derogatory remarks about rampant materialism are commonplace today. Money is very important because we live in a market society; practically anything you might want is for sale. Some things like drugs, or human beings, or sexual favors, or weapons, are not supposed to be for sale but they can be bought like food or clothes or medieval manuscripts. If you want to buy anything or if you want to secure someone's services, you will be asked for money. Everything has monetary value, as when someone sues for a large sum of money for wrongful death or a botched surgical procedure. Monetary value is placed on the loved one whom you have lost to a medical error. Money acquires supreme importance.

Some persons are suspicious of the market society because they think that money is somehow dirty, that it corrupts, or that interest in money is "crass or vulgar." In relation to alienation, however, the problem of money lies elsewhere. According to Marx,

> [T]he properties of money are my own (the possessor's) properties and faculties. That I am and *can do* is, therefore, not at all determined by my individuality. I *am* ugly but I can buy the most beautiful woman for myself. Consequently I am not *ugly*, for the effect of ugliness, the power to repel, is annulled by money. . . . I am *stupid*, but . . . can buy talented people for [my]self, and is not he who has power over the talented more talented than they? (Marx 1963:191; original emphasis)

I can be beautiful if I have the best clothes, expensive haircuts, a face-lift, perhaps, and can pay for stunning lovers. My limited intelligence need not be a hindrance if my speechwriters are brilliant and the author of my autobiography is talented. If only I had a fancy car, a big house, and belonged to a really nice club, I would have friends and be popular. If only I could pay for a fine private school to educate my children, they could go to a first-rate college and law school and have happy lives. In whatever way I may be natively deficient, if I have the money I can buy remedies to compensate for the excellences nature did not bestow on me. Money seems to have the power to make me anything I would like to be.

Marx exaggerates. My speechwriters, my advisers, the author of my autobiography do not make *me* intelligent. I still *am* the same person with limited intelligence, a small vocabulary, and feeble jokes. But money can change my *appearance*. I can seem more insightful and eloquent if someone writes a fine speech for me. I may appear to have depth that those who know me well have never discovered, if my autobiographer makes up the right stories about my life. Money cannot change me, but it can change the impression I leave. If I seek money above all, I seek not to change myself but to gain the means for managing how the world perceives me. In a world where money is thought to be the means to a good life, where we believe that if only we had the money we would be loved, could take pride in ourselves, and do great things, appearances come to count for a great deal.

Money will procure necessities—food, shelter, clothing. In simple societies such goods, if not grown at home, can be bartered in the marketplace or bought for money. But as societies become more complex, money and what it will buy acquire social significance. Possessions confer status. But substantial virtues are not for sale. I cannot buy wisdom or courage or a gentle soul; but I can buy the means for appearing wise or brave or kindly. There the pursuit of money is central, everyone cultivates appearances and, therefore, also practices deception. If they have money, persons with average endowments will try to deceive us into thinking that they are deep thinkers; the unlettered will pretend to be educated by flaunting the names of prestigious schools they managed to attend or filling their bookshelves with sets of leather-bound tomes they will never open. All want to seem knowledgeable when they are not and appear important by claiming close connections to well-known personages. They want us to think that they are powerful because their cars are. What matters is the impression they make on others, not whether the impression is accurate. On the contrary, it is all the better if they deceive others into being impressed by qualities they do not, in fact, possess. In a world ruled by the pursuit of money, deception is commonplace. The temptation to deceive is strong when appearances are so important and all try to appear other than they are. Everyday there are stories about important political personages who lied about their military record, about their education. Advertisers who misrepresent their products are so routine that they no longer appear in the news.

Emma's neighbor, the pharmacist Homais, is a shameless self-promoter and hustler. He persuades Bovary to try an operation on the lame stable boy. Instead of curing the deformity, the operation brings on an infection and the leg needs to be amputated. Homais takes no responsibility for this failure but instead tries to ingratiate himself with the famous surgeon who comes to perform the amputation. Later he promises to cure the blindness of a harmless idiot roaming the countryside. That cure, too, fails and Homais hounds the authorities to shut the poor half-wit up in a public institution to cover his own incompetence. The book ends with Homais being awarded the *Legion d'Honeur*, the much-coveted honor he had been pursuing tirelessly. Homais is recognized as an important citizen because he managed appearances skillfully—never mind that he was an incompetent windbag. Emma, who wanted to break through the appearances to a life of her own that counted for something, dies at her own hand.

Such a world is open to moral criticism for making it difficult to be upright and honest. But, in connection with alienation, mutual deception as an everyday occurrence creates different problems.

The Price of Cultivating Appearances

The eagerness to create good impressions, even at the cost of deceiving others, arises from the thought that if others saw us as we are, they would not pay attention to us because we are such insignificant persons. They would not want to be seen in our company or consider being our friends because we are, behind the fronts we present to the world, neither likable nor attractive. The eagerness to appear other than we are denigrates our selves. As we are manipulating appearances, we confess our inadequacy and thereby seriously weaken our own self-esteem. Weak self-esteem, in turn, makes it harder to resist the temptation to misrepresent ourselves.

Emma Bovary wanted what everyone wants—friends to treasure her company, to understand her, and to share her interests and concerns. She wanted to find a setting in which she was recognized for the energetic, intelligent, persistent person she was, who would be liked and sometimes loved. Such love and friendship are needed to legitimize the kind of life each of us has chosen. Triters need readers and publishers in order to be recognized as writers. Each of us needs others—either individuals or groups—to confirm who we are, to legitimate our sense of ourselves and how we present ourselves to the world. The athlete needs a team that lets her play; the violinist needs an orchestra. Poetry that no one reads is of dubious merit and its author a very marginal poet, at best. One's story about oneself depends on mutual recognition, on friendship, on love, on a variety of group relations in which we see and are seen more or less as we are. Emma needed others to recognize that she was a passable pianist and drew nicely; she needed someone to share her interest in books. Lacking such companions, she needed to gain the strength from others to be able to lead a life of her own—perhaps more solitary than she would have liked, but nevertheless significant—by occupying herself with work worth doing. But such firm self-esteem was difficult to achieve where everyone was maneuvering to appear in the best light. The self-denigration implicit in the constant posturing of the money society affected her. Always acting in order to create a good impression left her distant from others and made real friendship impossible. On stage all the time, as it were, she was separated from others by the footlights. We can *pretend* to be friends and lovers, but such relationships do not build selves. The constant practice of deception disrupts the mutual recognition that builds self-esteem.

We gain a sense of our own efficacy when others yield to our requests, a sense of our intelligence when others listen to us as we speak. We learn that we are desirable from being desired, and know that we can love when others blossom in our love. One's sense of one's own ability, value, and power develops slowly as one grows up and constructs a complex network of relationships. A world where others can be trusted teaches us confidence. Deceptive relationships, on the other hand, do not foster self-knowledge or self-esteem. Seeing oneself reflected in the eyes and acts of others, one learns to know and to be oneself. It is much harder to develop a self if those others are unreliable witnesses. When deception is common, it is difficult to accept the self that others mirror back. Self-esteem is then much harder won. It is difficult to learn to move confidently in a world where one must keep glancing over one's shoulder to see what others say and do when one's back is turned. In such a confusing world, persons cannot reach clarity about themselves.

Faint Friendships, Tepid Love

Distrust spreads isolation. In Emma's world, where everyone tries to impress everyone else, human relations are arid, and that adds to her misery. In a world dominated by appearances, love is, as often as not, counterfeit; the lovers are acting out a familiar ritual. The men Emma loves pretend to love her and she, at times when her passion falters, puts on dazzling displays as much to persuade herself that love can last as to reassure Leon or Rodolphe. Emma's beauty and her passionate energy move both of them, but not to love. Her affairs end in disaster because they are always, in part, theatrical performances, operatic extravaganzas. When the opera comes to Rouen with Lucia di Lammermoor, Emma leaves the opera house early because she gets bored. Her own passionate performances are more thrilling than the actors' intrigues on the stage.

But if love is only a performance, it does not nurture; it does not fill the soul with happiness, or allow one to take pride in one's person. It does not justify the conviction that one's life has meaning and that one is valuable because one is valued.

Competition and the Power to Keep Oneself Safe

It is more difficult to feel safe when deception is commonplace. It is reasonable to be on one's guard against those who do not hesitate to mislead. In Emma Bovary's world, as in ours, one must be ready to defend oneself against hidden threats. To protect oneself against harm from those who manage to deceive, one needs to seek the power to preserve oneself. If I must always see to my own protection, I will be extremely reluctant to cede any power I may have to anyone else.

From the very beginning, the concept of power has been central in these reflections about alienation. The alienated feel powerless because the world in which they find themselves allows them few opportunities to have their way. Human lives are not controlled by us but are buffeted by accident and the unforeseen. Confidence that one can have an effect on others is not easily achieved, and alienation is shot through with distrust of others—they do not care for me—and of oneself—I cannot make others care for me or take me seriously. Being oneself, owning one's life to an extent, holding past, present, and future together, as well as giving one's life some meaning—all that requires a certain amount of power. The power needed here is the ability to be efficacious, not the power to dominate other people. The desire to dominate others is often an expression of lack of efficacy in one's own life. Power as efficacy is lacking in alienation; one cannot make oneself felt or heard.

Thinly disguised power struggles are woven into Emma's romantic relations. Rodolphe is taken aback by the many valuable presents Emma gives him. "These presents however humiliated him; he refused several; she insisted and he ended by obeying, thinking her tyrannical and over exacting" (p. 388). More important, once she makes great demands on his devotion to her by wanting him to elope with her, he knows that she desires ties and therefore power over him, which he is not willing to yield to her. He leaves her abruptly. With Leon she plays the dominant role; at times she addresses him as "my child"; she fantasizes that she would like to supervise his life in minute detail. Power struggles are concealed in the heart of love. When Emma is in serious financial trouble she is reluctant to tell her husband Charles about it, for fear that it would give him the upper hand in their relationship. It is essential to remain in control.

The world Flaubert castigates in his portrait of Emma Bovary and her unhappy loves—a world he dismissively calls "bourgeois"—is a barren world. Everyone wants more money, and the power it brings, and, because of that, money is scarce; there can never be enough if everybody always wants more. All are condemned to compete for the limited wealth there is and the prestige it brings. The best competitors thrive and those who, like Emma, want love and an exuberant existence lose out in the midst of the schemers who, like Homais or L'Heureux, never hesitate to advance themselves shamelessly at the expense of others. Distrust is the undertone of many if not all human relations, and everyone is forced to see to their power, if only for self-preservation. Competition aggravates the distances between persons. Being safe, trusting, confident, and, most of all, opening oneself to the other in love are very precarious in the bourgeois society. Everyone is a possible competitor and no one is safe.

There are, of course, different kinds of competition that have different objectives—doing as well as possible in some cases, winning at any price in others. Two persons running spur each other on to a better performance. They compete, but they also encourage each other because the one running faster will inspire the other to do the same. Such a competition is coupled with mutual respect and concern for the other's well-being

(Davion 1987). At the other end of the scale is war—another kind of competition where the goal is the other's death. The footrace may end up without a clear winner (Longino 1987), or one may come in second and still be glad to have run so well. But if winning is all that matters, rather than an exceptional performance, one needs above all to eliminate the opponent from the competition, by any means necessary. Tinning is then more important than doing well. Whether it be in war or in capitalist competition, one augments one's holdings at another's expense in whatever way one can. Making your business larger and more prosperous than the competition may be due to skill and inventiveness, or to shady dealings, threats, bullying and violence, mistreating workers, deceptive advertising. Similarly in war: As long as you can gain victory, it matters not whether you win by bravery or treachery (McMurtry 1991).

It is difficult to gain mutual recognition in situations where destructive competition is always possible. If two persons compete for a job, a business contract, or someone's love, they will both try to understand the strength and weaknesses of their competitor. The more one knows about one's competitor, the better one will be able to exploit his weaknesses or counter his strengths. But no mutual relationship is established as long as each is trying to take something important away from the other. If competition is amicable and aims merely to make both competitors perform better, then each is interested in the other's excellence and will acknowledge and recognize the competitor's strengths, in order to bolster his performance. But not so where the competition is destructive and aims to deprive another person of something he wants very badly, be that power, or money, or social advancement. In situations where destructive competition is always possible, it is difficult to establish relations of mutual recognition.

Isolation

Constant competition breeds isolation. Everyone in Emma's world, as much as in ours, is very much alone. Flaubert draws a pitiless portrait of the small towns where Emma lives. There is no community and there are no group efforts. We hear of no community improvement efforts, no association for sports or other leisure activities, for the improvement of dairy herds, or for agricultural methods. There is no group to support a library, no collection of persons to agitate for this local project or that. The parish has not organized any prayer groups, or groups to beautify the church or decorate the altar. There are no burial societies or self-help groups. People do not come together informally to help out when one family encounters serious difficulties, when a road needs to be cleared or a bridge shored up. No wonder that in such an atomized setting, everyone feels very much alone. Nor is it surprising that those who are thus isolated have difficulties living lives of their own, or taking pleasure in life and thinking that it has some meaning. They end up with weak and indistinct selves that group membership is bound to threaten. Here groups are a threat to individual members because most are too unclear about their identity to be able to resist group pressures. One cannot see beyond such isolation to alternative group structures that do not engulf the individual person but thrive on the recognition of differences and the distinct contributions from different members. One's freedom in such a society is, as we shall see in the final chapter, quite incomplete.

That Was Then . . .

The story of Emma Bovary is set in the middle of the nineteenth century in rural Normandy. We are living 150 years later in mostly urban, highly industrialized Western countries. Does the poignant description of alienation in this story still apply to us? How is Emma's condition, even if we recognize it as our own, connected to capitalism, to markets, to the global economy?

Before considering those connections, we need to remind ourselves of the important difference between alienation, on the one hand, and oppression and exploitation, on the other, because those sets of concepts are frequently confused. Tremendous discrepancies in power exist in a capitalist society, where some people own and control productive resources, and others work for wages. The owners of productive resources determine whether the rest have work or not, and thus whether they live or die. The workers do not have comparable power over the owners. This discrepancy in economic power, mirrored in the disproportionate political power of large corporations or business groups in the democratic process, is often called "oppression." The discrepancy between the economic and political power of employers and that of employees manifests itself in sharp inequalities in income and wealth.[3] Capitalism, reigning unfettered, steadily increases disparities between the rich and the poor. That discrepancy is the result of exploitation.[4]

Alienation differs from oppression and exploitation. Oppression refers to disparity in power used by the more powerful to dominate the weaker. Exploitation manifests itself in the growing income gap between the poor and the rich. Alienation, the effect of the same conditions that produce oppression and exploitation, saps the energies for self-assertion, for developing trust in oneself and in others, for participating actively in the groups to which one belongs and facing difficulties courageously, for being resilient in the face of failures and living life, even when it is hard, with a modicum of cheerfulness. Alienation leaves us fearful, anxious not to be different from others, eager to conform and to be accepted. We are looking for diversions, for fun, living mostly in the present if we do not depreciate the present by comparing it with a better future forever over the horizon. Alienation weakens the personality and our ability to live good lives.

A signal feature of capitalism is the ever-widening scope of the marketplace. More and more goods—valued things, situations, relations, thoughts, melodies—become commodities. They are no longer made by men and women for their own use but are produced, often in gigantic quantities, to be sold to consumers in the marketplace. This vast extension of the commodity society has two important effects: As consumers of many commodities our lives change significantly and more importantly we change ourselves.

Commodification

Since human beings are embodied, lives take place in physical space and time and material objects are essential constituents of our personal identities. This is most obvious when we express ourselves in the things we create. The rooms we arrange for ourselves, the clothes we choose, the foods we prepare give public expression to our nature. We discover ourselves in what we make and own, and so do others. Things "become a sort of extension of a man's organs, the constant apparatus through which he gives reality to his ideas and wishes" (Syfers 2000:153). Identities are partly created in the arranging of one's material environment. Christopher Lasch (1984:31) quotes the philosopher Hannah Arendt as saying that "the things of this world have the function of stabilizing human life and their objectivity lies in the fact that . . . men, their ever changing nature notwithstanding, can retrieve their sameness, that is their identity, by being related to the same chair and the same table." The house I live in may have been built as one of a series of identical homes in a subdivision. But after a while, if I am a person in my own right, my house will reflect who I am. It will really be the house of my family and show in various ways that we have lived in it, that it has sheltered us and is the stage on which portions of our life unfold. The clothes everyone wears are mass-produced, but different people wear their clothes in different ways. The pair of shoes I have worn for many years are worthless on the market, but I treasure them and wouldn't think of throwing them out in order to replace them with a new pair of boots. They have become a part of my life and of who I am.

The consumer society has come in for a good deal of criticism—much of it deserved. It is wasteful; it is not sustainable; it is disturbed by invidious inequalities (Schor 2000). But it also infects life with impersonality; it makes us strangers in our own home and to ourselves. There the pressure is unrelenting to purchase *new* commodities, to have *new* clothes, a *new* house, a *new* car, all are urged to divest themselves of the physical embodiments of their past existence and to replace them with new things that are indistinguishable from everyone else's new things. With new things, we become, to an extent, new persons; and bereft of our history, we become as interchangeable with other persons as those new things are interchangeable with one another. Replacing our materiality we lose a significant portion of our identity. Instead of living in *our* house we live in spaces as neutral as hotel rooms, bare of any signs of human habitation. When everyone is constantly urged to acquire a new material existence, everyone's personality withdraws from the physical world and becomes that much more indistinct. Instead of being embodied in our personal things, we are (dis)embodied in impersonal commodities.

The market society recommends solving problems by buying commodities. If the doctor recommends that one lose weight, one goes and buys a large exercise machine. If one longs for comfortable evenings with friends, one has a bar built in one's basement. But since that does not bring in the sorts of friends one wants, the bar becomes the home for the unused exercise machine. Making things oneself, growing one's own vegetables, making one's own clothes does not make a lot of economic sense. It is not cost-effective. The commodity society discourages doing for oneself. One gets into the habit of buying goods and services instead of trying to solve one's problems with the means at hand. Emma's romanticism reflects that disempowerment of the individual. When Emma first realizes that Charles is not the love of her life, she thinks that if they could travel to exotic places perhaps their love would also be more extraordinary. And when she later fantasizes about her elopement with Rodolphe, she again thinks in great and splendid detail about the romantic landscape in which their love will flourish. Never does she think about what she and Rodolphe will *do* to maintain their happiness; for in a world where money speaks so loudly and incessantly, happiness does not flow from what we do or how we fashion ourselves and our lives, it flows from the commodities we can purchase. Emma dreams of the perfect love by imagining herself wealthy in a faraway place, in Paris, or in a distant tropical country, where the ambiance is just right for the perfect relationship. Her love is not

hers but depends on money that gives access to the life in exquisitely romantic locales. The setting is everything, and only money will take you there.
Happiness emanates from things one can buy, from luxuries that only money
can procure. When Emma is unhappy, it is easy for the unctuous L'Heureux
to tempt her with expensive purchases—a gothic prie-dieu at one time, filmy
scarves at another. It is this covetousness, the need to buy new things, that finally brings her downfall, when L'Heureux forecloses on the now considerable debt Emma owes him. The reliance on commodities tends to disempower persons. They are less inclined to do for themselves than to go out and
buy something or hire someone else's expertise. Because the expert is always
someone else, one loses the capacities needed to lead a life of one's own. Life
is something to be consumed rather than to be lived energetically; love is an
experience that one falls into rather than a relationship one sustains actively
and thoughtfully. Happiness is a rare gift rather than an accomplishment because the battle against alienation is never-ending. Commodities make us passive and thereby disempower us. They encourage alienation.

Self-Commodification

The second effect of the extension of production for the market and the consumption of commodities is a change in all of us: "[T]he worker conceives of
himself and/or his labor power as a mere commodity" (Arnold 1990:46). As
we think of ourselves, so we are. Human beings determine who they are, in
part, by forming images of themselves. We enact that self-understanding by
adopting particular roles. For this reason, progressive schools praise their students generously in the hope that the children, convinced of their exceptional
abilities, will turn in outstanding performances. For similar reasons, oppression
impairs the capacity to function in the world—not only because it causes
great pain but also because its victims internalize oppression and are incapac-
itated by their belief that they can do very little. Our understanding of our relationships to other human beings manifests itself in what we do with and to
others. We act like the commodity we think we are. The progressive commodification of society includes human beings: We too become commodities
and in this consists one more aspect of our alienation.

Commodities are intended for sale; they entice us to buy them. The message written all over them is "Buy me." To the extent that human beings
transform themselves into commodities, they too are at pains to look as good
as they can so that they will please. The intense interest in appearances, sati-
rized by Marx in his essay on money and castigated by Flaubert in his novel
of small-town life, exemplifies that commodification of human beings. We

no longer live to be ourselves in the groups to which we belong, where we are recognized and, sometimes, appreciated for who we are, but instead carefully design our appearances so to please others, most often persons unknown to us. Self-identity is less important than attracting strangers.

Observers of our world have noticed the overwhelming importance of appearances. The concern for how one appears to others displaces efforts to be oneself. Eduardo Galeano documents our mania for constructing impressive fronts in their most bizarre form:

> "In the Fall of 98, in the center of Buenos Aires, an inattentive pedestrian was hit by a bus. The victim was crossing the street while talking on a cell phone. Thile talking? While pretending to be talking: she was holding a toy telephone" (Galeano 1998:258).

Galeano entitles this story "A Martyr." The woman is a martyr to appearances, to pretending to be sufficiently affluent to own a cell phone. Needing to seem affluent when all she could afford was a plastic toy, needing to seem engrossed in an important call in the middle of a busy street, this woman dies a martyr to the tyranny of appearances.

With mass culture comes the phenomenon of the "fan." Fans create their lives and a whole subculture around admiration for an actor or actress, a rock band, or a race car driver. The fan's self is a derivative of someone famous. I am someone because I am engrossed in the life of a celebrity. My selfhood does not depend on the self of another person, but only on the image presented in fan magazines. The fan's self-identity is a derivative of the media image of another person who is, in fact, unknown. Fans dream of being picked out of a crowd by their hero. They would suddenly be a special person because their favorite singer asked them to come onstage in front of all the other fans. Singled out by the famous performer in front of the crowd, the lucky fan acquires, if only for a moment, a unique identity (Lewis 1992). Self-identity is constructed out of appearances not only in the world of Emma Bovary but also in our own. Nor is this only true in the world of popular culture. Highbrows are just as eager to shake the hand of the famous author or to catch a smile from the piano virtuoso. Who would not get a lift from having Bill Gates answer their question at a public forum?

Wage Work

In a money economy, work for wages becomes the rule; the ability to work becomes a commodity. Control over the wage worker is vested in the employer, who is intent on maintaining that control. Even where worker and employer work well together, the underlying relation is one of conflict over control of work. Trust is not easily acquired in this setting. Nor is it easy to learn to approach one's work confident that one will do well because the judgment about that is in the hands of others with whom one has a structurally conflictual relationship.

Where wage work is the rule, the employer's interest is in paying wages that are as low as possible. Thus there is an interest in investing in complex machines that make the worker into a minimally skilled machine minder so that many workers will have skills easily learned in a day or so. Work does not allow them the pride of being skillful. What is more, when the complex machine malfunctions, the low-skill machine minders cannot fix it. Their work does not contribute to their confidence in their own ability to manage their world (Sennett 1998).

Good health requires that one's life be important and that one's activities serve important purposes; indeed, research shows that workers who have more control in their work lead healthier lives (Steptoe et al. 1993; Wickrama et al. 1995). But work for pay is work for the sake of money. The work itself maybe quite insignificant—to sell more hula hoops, to enrich the shareholders of a company unknown to the workers, to make one's boss look good in the eyes of her boss in turn. There one works for money, one chooses the work by the pay and not primarily by its importance. What one actually does at work is up to the employer and not due to one's own choices as to what is worth doing and what is not. Work can contribute to a sense of importance in one's life, but it often does not do so where wage work is the rule and only the money paid for working matters.[5]

But wage work involves even more insidious commodification of persons, because workers need to procure work in the first place. The day laborer standing in the street to be hired for a day's work needs to look alert and strong. The college student going for a job interview needs to dress up and present him- or herself as well-trained, cooperative, and well-groomed. The academic researcher, pressured by the university to bring in research money, has to present projects that foundations are prepared to fund. One needs to turn oneself into an attractive and enticing commodity in order to procure work. The first interviews are often brief; it is all-important to make a good impression.

In all but the most menial work, one must have the right preparation. Self-commodification for the labor market infects education. The purpose of education, at best, is to enrich lives. But in a capitalist society, the purpose of education is to prepare one for getting a good job. One goes to college in order to package oneself attractively for future employers. Almost all college students suffer from this conflict between learning something that will deepen their understanding of their own life and person, and getting good grades and a respectable degree to impress prospective employers in the future. For the respectable degree, one needs to impress one's professors so that they will dispense good grades. In preparation for impressing future employers, students are trained in their college classes to scope out what the professor expects of them and to deliver that product to the "customer."

Someone may agree with the foregoing analysis but remind us that human beings, as we saw in the preceding chapter, are not all of one piece. Most of us have several personalities that in various ways conflict with each other. So it may well be true that we pay a great deal of attention to how we appear to others insofar as we are employees or potential employees. But, the critic continues, we have many lives and our life as employees is only one of those. We have lives as sons and daughters, as mothers and fathers, as friends. We have many different interests to fill our leisure. We are neighbors, co-workers, members of unions, teachers to our students; we lead Boy Scout troops, or sing in barbershop quartets. In these different aspects of our lives we are not commodified; there is no pressure to cultivate attractive appearances. On the contrary, it matters a great deal that as children or as parents, as friends or as lovers, we have firm self-identities and let ourselves be seen as we are.

This criticism presents a serious difficulty. It suggests that Flaubert's picture is one-sided, or overdrawn. Marx may be right about the effects of money, but money is not everything. The critic of wage work may be right in saying that it is not only oppressive and exploitative but also tends to distort our character. But not all our life has to do with money, with making or spending it. We do not spend all day at work. And there's plenty of room to build a clear self-identity after-hours.

All this is true and an important reminder that human lives and personalities are very complicated and subject to many different conflicting forces. It is a grand oversimplification to say that capitalism alienates. Instead we need to say that wage work and the efforts necessary to obtain wage work weaken our personalities, but that there are other spaces, other possibilities, other demands that may well induce us to develop lives and identities of our own. But human lives do not neatly separate into wage work that alienates, on the one hand, and the rest of our lives that give us scope for developing self-identities, on the other. Pressures to appear attractive extend beyond the workplace. Spreading out from wage work, the obsession with how one appears penetrates through most of daily life.

Additional forces push us toward commodifying ourselves. Body parts and bodily functions have become marketable commodities. There is a live trade in blood and body parts—a good deal of it illegal, but for all that just as real as any other form of trade. The ability to bear children is for sale; so is human sperm. Even healthcare is a commodity, and those with no money have a greater chance to die young. Human life itself is, in that sense, for sale; my very existence, these years of later life and their productivity are mine because I'm fortunate enough to be able to pay for them. It is more difficult to resist the temptation to treat myself as a commodity if my body and some of its functions are also commodified.

Quite different but equally powerful is another aspect of the labor market. Not only do I have to make myself attractive to employers, as well as to teachers and others who may help me to secure work, but I have to make myself more attractive than my competitors. Competition is essential to market transactions; poor competitors will not get ahead. Operating in a market requires not only a certain repertoire of actions but also a certain kind of personality, one that is willing to injure others for the sake of one's own advancement. I noted earlier in this chapter the difference between benign and destructive competition (see "Competition and the Power to Keep Oneself Safe"). In the market, competition is destructive. The competitor needs to be eliminated, not spurred on to better performances. In order to do well in markets, one needs to give free reign to one's inclination to harm others and to suppress all tendencies to feel sympathy for their pain. For many people, the willingness to compete spreads to other parts of their lives. Men compete with each other by telling lies about their sexual exploits. Siblings compete for the affection of their parents; parents, for the affection of their children. The new father competes with the new infant for the mother's attention. Competitiveness is diffused throughout our lives. It oozes out from various markets and insinuates itself into many other facets of our lives.

Competitiveness also infects our thinking about selves and self-identity. In a society pervaded and, at times, dominated by competitions, it may well seem that ". . . we evaluate how *well* we do something by comparing our performance to others, to what others can do. . . . Self-esteem is based on *differentiating characteristics;* that's why it is *self*-esteem" (Nozick 1974:240–243; original emphasis). It seems, at first, plausible that self-esteem rests on comparisons with others, on doing better than others, on winning prizes, going to famous schools, getting jobs in prestigious institutions. One can be proud of being set apart from others by winning. But then we remember that there are different ways of differentiating oneself from others and that many of these do not build real self-esteem. The poor white sharecropper who consoles himself by saying "At least, I am not black" was not displaying his self-esteem; neither were the Jewish patriarchs who thanked God in their daily prayers for not creating them as women. Richard Yates, in his novel *Revolutionary Road,* describes a young couple whose work is tedious, their home in a new development tasteless, their friends uninteresting. They keep repeating to themselves, however, that they are "different from the common herd"—a desperate comparison that betrays nothing so clearly as their lack of self-esteem (Yates 1961). Difference is not a source of self-love. Self-esteem based on comparisons to others functions under the motto of "I may be worthless, but you are even more so." All of life has become a competitive arena; competition is no longer restricted to the workplace or the market.

In the competition for work, money, favors, love, fame, it matters that we appear more deserving, more able, more lovable than our competitors. It matters much less who we are. The pervasive atmosphere of competition furthers the inclination to manage appearances instead of building firm selves.

Capitalism is not just a set of institutions and structures; it is a living, functioning system. There are large numbers of people who not only participate in these institutions but actively promote them. Capitalism today mass-produces a dizzying array of commodities. But mass production requires mass consumption (Lasch 1978). Capitalist firms are not content just to produce goods; they need to market them. They need to persuade us to buy those goods and they do that by trying to tell us that in almost every area of our lives the products of industry will enhance our lives. The elegant car will win the love of the elegant woman. If that doesn't work, she will love you for the large house you buy. Clothes are there to impress others, to look "cool" or "attractive"; the products we buy are recommended as wrappings for the commodities we are. The consumer society is a society of appearances, of making impressions on others, of attracting attention and affection by our outsides. As consumers of commodities we have turned ourselves into commodities. Individual capitalists promote the commodification of people just as they promote their products.

But capitalist practices and the commodification of human beings are also promoted more abstractly by economists in the employ of large corporations and universities. Not content to study the functioning of actual markets, many of these economists make large claims that the model of the market fits all human transactions. Economic description of the market takes on ethical and political overtones when it prescribes how society should organize itself. At least one economist has earned a Nobel Prize for telling us that all human relationships are relationships in a marketplace and that all our interactions can be understood as exchanges of commodities (Becker 1986). And a judge has gained fame and fortune by reinterpreting the law on the model of the marketplace (Posner 1992). The pressure on us to think of ourselves as commodities and to be commodities extends far beyond the labor market.

As human beings, we seek lives that have meaning and that conform to our moral aspirations. As participants in the capitalist economy, we seek to maximize profit—regardless of whether in so doing we act morally or not. Our properly human aspirations are in conflict with capitalist practices and if the latter are extended to the full range of human activity, our humanity suffers (Luntley 1989). No wonder that alienation is rampant in our lives. Here are other manifestations of it.

Isolation Today

Our culture is only too aware of pervasive isolation but is also quite confused about it. On the one hand, poets, like Eliot, mourn this isolation profoundly:

> *I grow old . . . I grow old.*
> *I shall wear the bottoms of my trousers rolled.*
> *Shall I part my hair behind? Do I dare to eat a peach?*
> *I shall wear white flannel trousers, and walk upon the beach.*
> *I have heard the mermaids singing, each to each.*
> *I do not think that they will sing to me.* (Eliot 1963)

On the other hand, political theorists defending liberalism insist vociferously that human beings are and must be separate from one another (Kateb 1989). Being alone is the price of liberty. The theory behind this claim is familiar. In the course of their energetic polemics against conformism, Rousseau, Tolstoy, Nietzsche, and Heidegger insist that individuals can either give over their life to a group and take direction from it or be themselves by living apart like Zarathustra alone on his mountain. Being one's own person requires that one be autonomous and quite separate from all others. But this liberal view completely overlooks the difference between passive group membership—whereby the individual, submerged in the group and subordinated to its desires, leaves all important decisions to shadowy others—and active group membership—whereby one participates in shaping the ideals and activities of the group. The active participant is not conformist but creative. In contributing to the life of the group, active participants shape their own life as well as that of others. They submit to the group only insofar as they also contribute to it.[6]

Prevailing confusions about individuality are reflected in language. We use the word *group* to refer to any association of individuals, whether its members are actively contributing to the work and identity of the group or are more or less passive; whether the members are in the group as separate individuals trying to preserve their identity against encroachment by the group or find themselves and their identity in the memberships of various groups to which they contribute actively. Language does not allow us to differentiate easily between the members of a corporation working to enhance the value of the corporation but at the same time looking to enhance their own net worth and power at the expense of other members of the group and the corporation as a whole, on the one hand, and members of a group in which cooperation is in everyone's self-interest and public and private agendas are at a minimum, on the other. In this last case, group interest and private interest are much more closely coincident than in groups of temporarily cooperating competitors.

Such active group membership strengthens selves significantly. My opinions and choices are public; they are recognized by others, and are validated by merging with the choices made by the group at the end of collective deliberations. Different views, different attitudes, and different traits of persons enrich this public discussion. In an active community, one's difference counts and is known and rewarded. One gains self-esteem by gaining recognition for one's unique contribution to the group, made possible by one's differences from others. One gives one's life some meaning by participating in activities that seem worthwhile to a group of people who respect one and whose judgment one takes seriously.

The prevailing theoretical confusions about being an individual reflect the realities of the market society. The market society makes it difficult to work together to improve the world; separateness is indeed the prevailing mode of being. By encouraging destructive competition, it obstructs cooperative ventures. In the market, all try to enrich themselves individually; if we work together with others it is in the hope that each of us will end up wealthier or more powerful. Support for a common good is available only if each separate individual can hope for an individual advantage from working for it. Cooperation is defensible only as a means to individual enrichment. But cooperation tends to be short-lived. After enriching themselves by working together, participants in the market become bitter competitors in the next campaign for wealth and power (Holmstrom 2000).

To be sure, workplaces boast many teams, committees, working groups, and so on; however, these are not self-organized and more or less autonomous groups but are mandated by the higher-ups for specific purposes.[7] Here one still cooperates in pursuit of one's own advancement and in the hope of getting ahead of the competitors. Working in such groups is just one more form of wage work. One does what one is told, singly or in groups, but one is always taking orders and pursuing one's own interest, possibly at the expense of others. Outside of work, however, community groups, informal associations and networks are decaying sufficiently rapidly that social scientists have been able to document our progressive isolation. People visit less with neighbors and family; social networks are shrinking (Lane 2000). A noticeable drop-off has occurred in the memberships of bowling leagues, PTAs, and fraternal organizations. Fewer persons vote, and fewer voters attend political meetings (Putnam 1995).

The money economy, with its underlying competition and the isolation it breeds, reduces the strength that individual selves derive from being active participants in the life of groups. It becomes difficult and rare to be an *active* participant in a group. As a consequence, one's only hope seems to lie in intimate relations with one other person, as popular music repeats endlessly. But in such relations between individuals who are very isolated, constructing one's self is much more difficult than in lively and active groups. Isolation increases further by the more frequent failure of couple relations.

Time

There are different kinds of time. One kind is time as an episode in life, a set of experiences that we refer to afterward as "good times" or "hard times," as in the famous first line of *A Tale of Two Cities:* "It was the best of times; it was the worst of times" (Dickens 2000). Times, in that sentence, refer to periods in a life as one lives it, and to the actions and experiences of those periods. This is time identified by what happens, what one does, how one responds, and what one learns. It is time in a sense very different from clock time—time as quantitative, as measured in seconds, minutes, days. Every second is like every other second; none has any content, none is good or bad, or hard or easy. Minutes when I am asleep are no different from those filled with important events. They are just small segments of duration as counted by a particular kind of machine, a clock.

What happens in our lives, whether the times are good, or easy, or hard, or terrifying, is of supreme importance. But clock time matters too, of course: how long one's life lasts, how much more time one has left. Still, how much clock time remains available is important only in relation to what one can do in that time, to the actions or events that fill it. It is hard to die when you feel that your life has been empty and you never did what you set out to do, or an important project has not yet been completed. The importance of clock time depends on the quality of the life whose duration is being measured. If a project fails or proves to be useless, then time—quantitative time—has been wasted. It is a waste of time to try to interpret an unintelligible text, to spend days in a drunken stupor, or to be hurtful and destructive.

For a society obsessed with money, the value of clock time, of minutes, hours, or days, is no longer the quality of that time, the actions or events that fill it. Now time becomes a commodity; it can be bought or sold. Now "time is money." That commodity is quantitative time, time that has no intrinsic content but is valuable as a means to some end, primarily the making of money. Days, hours, seconds are used well when we make lots of money; they are wasted when we do not produce anything of monetary value.

With commodification, clock time gains importance. Tasting time becomes a serious matter; it becomes inconceivable that one spends days without making money or laying the foundation for future profits. Less emphasis is put on qualitative time, on the content of one's life. Saving time becomes a concern when one does not ask whether the saved time will be used for great deeds or will be frittered away. Implicit in the entire way of thinking that takes quantitative time so seriously is that time saved will be used to produce more wealth. In a society focused on making money, clock time becomes primarily important as a means of making money. It becomes important to be efficient, to earn as much as possible in the shortest amount of time. Just being, playing games, watching the grass grow, or the eagles circling lazily above a mountain meadow—all that is wasting time. Things that don't make money, such as playing the guitar to entertain oneself and one's friends, telling stories, or just daydreaming, are now looked down upon as irresponsible because they do not turn a profit. Nothing is being accomplished by way of enriching oneself. It is no longer enough just to *be*. But if everything we do serves some other purpose and must show some profit, then no events or experiences are worthwhile in themselves. Thus, in the end, nothing matters.

Michael Ende's *Momo* displays chillingly a society where "time is money" and everyone is rushing to save time, to accomplish more in less time: Into a world that functions quite well and provides people with different but, on the whole, happy lives comes an army of gray men who urge everyone to save time because time is valuable and should not be wasted. Their message induces more and more people to stop living the leisurely lives they enjoy and to begin hustling to save time, to be efficient and not waste precious minutes in idle conversation, in simple acts of kindness:

> Admittedly time savers were better dressed. . . . They earned more money and had more to spend, but they looked tired, disgruntled and sour. . . . Whatever the occasion, whether solemn or joyous, time savers could no longer celebrate it properly. Daydreaming they regarded as almost a criminal offense. . . . It had ceased to matter that people should enjoy their work and take pride in it; on the contrary, enjoyment only slowed them down. (Ende 1974:59)[8]

Holding your child, weeding the garden, writing a book are no longer good ways to spend your time, unless you can justify them as means to something else. But is that something else good? Time commodified comes to resemble money in that it has no intrinsic value but serves only as a means to obtain other goods. But if the means absorb all our attention because we only want more money, and worry that we are wasting time, then it becomes harder and harder to explain what all this effort is for. What will be accomplished with all the time saved? What benefits will accrue from the money we have accumulated with such exemplary industriousness? It is not easy to find an answer to these questions, for the pleasures of life, of companionship, of cooperation, of play and laughter have all been banned unless they generate money. The busy accumulators of money, the careful savers of time, have turned away from the things that make life meaningful and thus they end up rich but their lives are hard to make sense of. With all their money they can only buy more commodities; but they cannot buy a meaning for their life. They cannot hire someone to make sense of their life. ("Can't buy me love.") The time savers and money makers cannot find what is most important—a life that is to some extent coherent. The commodification of time is one more obstacle in the way of making sense of one's life, so that it counts for something and has a purpose. Time spent only to gain the means for ends, without attending to ends themselves, leaves one with a life that has no meaning and thus spreads alienation. By giving exaggerated importance to clock time, the society fixated on money spreads alienation.

The Economics of Conformity

In the market society, the value of things becomes identified with their price. People express their approval of the work of an amateur painter by saying "This stuff is good. It must be worth money," or they wait to see if the work brings a significant price in the market before they pronounce it good. Even economists overlook the fact that what brings a high price in the market often is not really valuable. The market misjudges values. One claim of economics is that each agent's remuneration will be proportionate to his or her contribution. But

> [a] social system that sets artists to shining shoes and pays them what they are worth in that occupation is no less open to condemnation than one that sets them to work at their art and pays them what they would be worth as bootblacks. . . . The product or contribution is always measured in terms of price, which does not correspond closely with ethical values . . . " (Knight 1935:55)

because price depends on demand and demand is manipulated by the economic system. But what matters in human lives is that their life be meaningful, that it have value for them. They do what is important to them. There value and importance are equated with price, and price is determined by the market, it is more difficult to live life in ways that are valuable to the individual—particularly if what is important to the individual has little or no market value. What is valuable to individuals depends on how they construct their lives and the community in which they live. The value of all actions, events, and objects depends on a specific group of people and their relations to one another. Prices, on the other hand, depend on the impersonal mechanisms equilibrating supply and demand. When values are confused with prices, we find ourselves vacillating between what is worth time and effort to us and what we should prize according to the dictates of the market. The result is serious confusion about what is important to each one of us.

In such a society, it becomes more difficult to make life one's own, to make sense of it and form it into an intelligible story. It becomes more difficult to choose what the market deems worthless, because in so doing one is thought to waste one's precious time—and, living in this society, one finds it well-nigh impossible not to feel that wasting time is a great sin. Refusing what the market prizes highly is similarly difficult. It appears utterly irrational. The market does not coerce us, but its pressure is significant and not easy to resist.

If money is all-important, choices must be "rational": I must get as much for my money as possible. Things without fixed monetary value tend to be slighted. Baking my own bread or growing my own vegetables is clearly not cost-effective. The bread I buy is liable to be better than what I bake myself, and it is bound to be cheaper. The time I spend with my children is more expensive, if I am a high-priced professional, than the time of a paid caretaker. There exists no convincing evidence that my absence will harm them. Economists acknowledge that one may, for reasons all one's own, be willing to pay a premium for a good that is exorbitantly expensive, such as homemade bread, home-grown tomatoes, or nightly reading to one's children. But in the market society the pressure is unrelenting to buy cheap and sell dear. Goods are cheap if mass-produced, and mass-production responds to widespread demand. The market puts pressure on each of us to want what others want, because being produced in large quantities it is cheaper and hence often a more rational choice.[9]

> Diversity is the enemy of profitability; uniformity is in command. Mass-production on a gigantic scale imposes on all parties its compulsory standards of consumption. This dictatorship of a compulsory imposition of uniformity . . . reproduces human beings as photocopies of the exemplary consumer. (Galeano 1998:260; my translation)

The centrality of money and commercialism enforces conformity to a set of choices that are widely preferred and thus can be satisfied more economically than choices that may well depart from those of the majority (Lasch 1978). Moreover, advertisers often manipulate those choices carefully and ingeniously. Economic rationality pushes us toward life choices that are determined by major corporations and away from decisions that would be more in keeping with the self we are constructing as we try to give some coherence to our lives. Here is one more pressure to leave the direction of one's life to others, to conform, rather than making choices that might make one's life more one's own and have some internal coherence. The market society advances alienation by pushing us toward conformity.

One symptom of alienation we considered in the preceding chapter (see "Self-Esteem") is that one has great difficulties trusting oneself to make good choices, to have sound judgment about what is important and what is not, and what is valuable in one's life and what is less so. To the extent that one lacks recognition, that one does not feel oneself confirmed and valued by others, the pressures of the market toward values held by the largest number of persons are irresistible. Equally difficult to resist are the forces that push us toward considering time only in money terms without having any sense of what it is good for. The alienated find it hard to resist the influences that aggravate alienation. Alienation breeds more alienation because it weakens our resistance to the forces of the market that alienate us.

You Can't Be Serious . . .

Capitalism alienates. But are there alternatives to capitalism? We are accustomed to raising that question globally by contrasting capitalism with socialism. The logic of the preceding argument then compels us to argue that socialism is needed in order to overcome alienation. Most readers, even if they have so far been sympathetic to the main thoughts in this book, will refuse to follow here because they know from the experience of the Soviet Union that socialism is a vain dream; the high hopes with which socialist experiments were undertaken in the last century have all been disappointed. The reality turned out to be much darker and more frightening than the dream.

In considering this question about alternatives to capitalism, we enter a large and complex field of many different debates to which I cannot do justice. I can only summarize very briefly the implications of this reflection about alienation for social change. (For more elaborate arguments about alternatives to capitalism, readers are urged to consult the works cited in the Recommended Reading list at the end of the book.)

It has been repeated endlessly, for many years, that socialism is impossible and, therefore, that there exists no alternative to capitalism. As a consequence, we have been told, we have to accept capitalism as it is because "there is no alternative." This line of argumentation presupposes that there is only one capitalism. But we would no more argue that all forms of capitalism are the same than we would assert that there is only one form of Christianity, or that all versions of Islam are essentially the same. There exist many different versions of Judaism. Similarly, there are many different kinds of capitalism. The form we experience today knows no limits. It penetrates every aspect of our lives. It uses its enormous power to smooth the way for more unlimited and uncontrolled capitalist practices everywhere. It brooks no criticism; it accepts no democratic controls from the citizenry or its elected representatives. But this is, in fact, an extreme version of capitalism.

There have been other versions that have tried, often successfully, to alleviate the worst abuses of unfettered capitalism. Capitalism, in its extreme form, has many different parts. These different parts may well be modified in the interest of the vast majority. It is not obvious that wage labor is essential; nor is it obvious that competition needs to extend to all areas of social life, or that all the goods available in the society must be for sale (Kenworthy 1990). These three assumptions are being actively challenged by the movement of cooperatives and worker-owned businesses (Krimerman and Lindenfeld 1992), by many different community groups that have tried to develop alternative forms of social interaction to competition (King 1963, Deming 1984), and by economists reflecting about the spread of commodification (Radin 1996).[10]

There is no clear reason for denying that such changes are possible. Whether they have any limits is not known at the moment. What we should call such a transformed capitalism is of little interest. If your first impulse is to say "It's impossible!" perhaps you need to remind yourself of what you just read and ask yourself whether this negative certainty is not just one more manifestation of alienation.

Summary

Why did Emma Bovary die? We can recount her story, but questions remain: Would her life have been happier if she had read fewer trashy romances, or if her mother had not died so early, or if she had been a less somber and negative person? We do not know with certainty what the causes of actions are—not of the actions of others, nor of our own. That uncertainty serves as a reminder of the precondition of alienation: Not only do we live in a world that is governed by accident, but we are never sure that we understand the events that affect us or what we do in response to those circumstances. At the same time, as thinking beings, we try to understand and to make some sort of sense of the lives we lead even if its separate parts are often unexpected and opaque.

Circumstances have a great deal to do with our ability to make our lives meaningful. Meaning is disrupted by great catastrophes, by excessive suffering, by sudden death. But the ability to find and create meaning also depends on whether social circumstances are favorable or whether they deprive us of the opportunities to learn how to live lives that make some sense. Emma Bovary's death may be due to bad luck, unfavorable circumstances, an unsuitable marriage, or the boredom of small-town life, but the market society clearly interferes with her efforts to make something of her life. With money central in everyone's calculations, deception is everywhere, as is competition, and both undermine self-esteem. The need to deceive others denigrates oneself as it distances friends and makes lovers distrustful of one another.

Mutual recognition is harder to come by when destructive competition is always threatening. Instead of making a life for oneself and those close by, one tends, in a market society, to look to commodities to heal wounds and solve problems and, finally, to turn oneself into a commodity. Passivity, helplessness, and incompetence are encouraged by the far-going commodification of social life. A world that is purchased is not one's own; in order to be at home in it we have to make a world for ourselves, not buy it ready-made. In the commodity society it is more difficult to feel at home and to feel that one has some, however modest, capacities to shape one's life. Isolated and discouraged, the inhabitants of the market society find their joys and griefs to be tepid, their friendships distant. It is extraordinarily difficult to find groups in which one can jointly build a better future in the pursuit of shared goals. A life derives meaning from continuous efforts or stances that one holds to be important. But when one works for money, not for the sake of the activity itself, and one's activity is always directed by the employer and serves that employer's ends, not one's own, that activity is deprived of intrinsic importance. When, ultimately, all activities are only means to a further end because time has become money and, like money, is useful only as a means to obtain other goods, then it is very hard to find and to hold onto goals that are important in their own right. To that extent, life is emptied of importance and becomes meaningless.

Stories like that of Emma Bovary are instructive because they make sense in ways that life does not. Stories, however complex and attuned to ambiguities, are still more simple than the real world. In our own world, where money is of supreme importance to so many persons, the landscape is nevertheless not as bleak as Flaubert's Norman countryside. Even in this most commercial of commercial cultures, not everyone is pretending all the time, without real friends, deprived of all sources of solid self-esteem. But the rampant commercialism does make it more difficult to learn how to live one's own life, how to find and to give recognition, how to dare to lead a life that is one's own in some respects or tell a story about oneself that makes sense without being an all-out lie. It makes it more difficult to trust, to suppress the impulse to compete and keep up one's guard; it makes it more difficult to maintain one's strength to resist the temptations of the market society. The economic "rationality" of the market does work to dissuade one from developing one's own tastes and standards, and from aiming for a life that has its own story.

Having eliminated group life, the market society isolates all and restricts relationships primarily to love and friendship with one other individual. Emma's yearning for the one great love is not just a sign of her romanticism but also reflects the individualism of her society where groups do not play a major role because everyone is pursuing individual profit and self-advancement. There exist few if any goals shared by groups. Few can strengthen their identity or sense of purposefulness by participating in the project that a group has undertaken and that the enthusiasm of individual members—different ones at different times perhaps—sustains. Since she can find recognition for her self from only one other person, poor Emma, married to a kindly dullard, has little hope for constructing a self. Then and now, the fixation on romantic love is an indication that few persons find themselves to be members of groups in which they participate actively, because the market society has pushed everyone to pursue individual advantage above all.[11]

The market society does not do well by us. In the end it reduces our ability to be truly free.

Notes

1. Obviously social conditions are not the only obstacles to overcoming the precondition of alienation. Some individuals are drained of energy by illness. Others grow up without a healthy sense of their own worth due to childhood abuse or political persecution. There are endless sources of weak selves and not all of them can be laid at the door of social systems.

2. Emma's dreaming illustrates the ambiguity of stories. They can often bear widely divergent interpretations. Her dreaming may be the expression of her will to have a life that matters and makes sense. It may also be an escape from the challenges that the precondition of alienation presents. This ambiguity does no harm. Different lessons can be drawn from the same story.

3. "Average total CEO compensation has increased by 442 percent since 1990, when the poor fellows only averaged $2 million a year. They now earn more than 400 times what their average worker makes, up from 40 times as much in 1980" (de Graaf et al. 2001:80).

4. The claim that capitalism exploits is extremely controversial, as is the definition of the concept of exploitation. What cannot be disputed, however, is the empirical fact that the triumphal march of capitalism in recent years has aggravated disparities in income (Arnold 1990).

5. Young persons are often exhorted to "be all they can be," but that, of course, means no more than that they should do the best they can under the present system of wage labor.

6. Rousseau's General Will acknowledges that life and work in groups are central to the well-being of the individual.

7. Readers may object to this characterization of the modern corporate workplace, pointing to the wide use of teams in production and services. But there are different kinds of teams, and the majority do no more than solicit employee opinion or allow management more personal access to individual workers. Only 2 percent of American workers participate in genuinely self-managed teams (Wellins et al. 1991:44). Most teams are management creations and remain tightly controlled by upper-level executives (Grenier 1988:18).

8. I am indebted for this reference to my son, Eli Schmitt.

9. This "rational choice" is, of course, strictly a matter of economic rationality. Economics contributes to widespread alienation by giving a "scientific" support to the claim that economic rationality is the only form of human rationality.

10. There has been a great deal of debate in recent years about different forms of capitalism and socialism and the feasibility of each. The debate began around the time of World War II. It has continued with a variety of different proposals for a less destructive capitalism as well as a socialism less brutal and inefficient than that of the Soviet Union (Roemer 1994; Schweickart 1993; van Parijs 1992).

11. It is tempting to respond to the claims made in this chapter by saying that they apply only to the middle class in highly technologically developed countries. Problems of consumerism do not plague the poor, so the objection goes, and the poor are the vast majority of people in most countries. But, of course, wage labor is the common lot of the poor, and the culture of consumerism plagues not only those with money to spend but also those who would like to consume but cannot. Poverty tends to bring its own form of alienation by restricting to a bare minimum the choices of how to live one's life. "The poor are taunted by television programs and commercials that flash before them images of consumption standards that are considered typical of the average American, but which they have no possibility of achieving" (de Graaf et al. 2001:82).

5

ALIENATION LIMITS FREEDOM

Judi Dubey's lovers had always been men who were married or otherwise committed. Being a therapist herself, she understood what that meant: She was unwilling to enter relationships that had no initial limits, that might demand of her complete openness and full engagement with another human being. But now, living with Laf, and being very ill, she discovers that he can be relied on, that he will not take advantage of her weakness, that he is no threat to her identity. That is an important discovery. She also learns that both she and Laf can maintain their own lives, their own personalities, and their divergent beliefs while living very closely to one another. Her bodily dependence does not make her less of a person in her own right; she need not give up her views of her life and of the world because she is unable to care for herself. In some ways she becomes a more independent person because she can accept Laf's help where needed and yet remain herself. She learns a love that is richer and more complex.

And so does Laf. After having looked for romantic love for twelve years, he is now finding that loving may have less to do with springtime and blooming lilacs and more with cooking, washing dishes, and nursing a very sick person gently and tenderly. Romantic love yearns to escape the everyday and Laf did just that by leaving the housework and the dishes to his wife Martha. But now love permeates the fabric of everyday life; it consists of the many small acts of kindness that daily life allows lovers. For him too, new forms of loving become possible. Both learn to love differently. Neither of them had set out to learn those lessons; circumstances forced that new knowledge on them. But they were fortunate that life allowed them to learn.

Growing up in a world where all tried to be agreeable, to get along, while trying to advance their own careers, Ivan Ilych also learns, once he falls ill, that there are other ways to live than to skim over the surface of life in order to offend no one. He discovers new questions about his life and choices to be made that he had not been clearly aware of. He discovers that lack of love is more devastating than loss of money, and that the simple openness and kindness shown him by his servant Gerasim is worth a great deal more than the clever conversation in polite society that he was accustomed to. Like Laf and Judi, he discovers new ways of living; he finds that he has choices previously unknown to him.

Emma Bovary cannot discover what she can do to give her life some meaning and coherence, however hard she tries. She can find no examples of lives different from her humdrum existence except the overheated romantic fantasies that she seeks to live out. In her society, where everyone craves money and personal advantage, common projects do not exist that would give her a firmer sense of being anchored in her world, of being a person of some importance with contributions to make. Constrained by her circumstances of living in a particularly grim society, she is unable to make her life her own, to live as she would wish. She is prevented from doing what she wants most, to make something of her life, to give some weight to her existence, to assert her abilities and her importance, to find recognition for who she is.

All four are struggling with the precondition of alienation, of being born into a setting that is neither chosen nor fully understood and yet wanting to live their lives deliberately to suit the body, the situation, and the personality with which fortune endowed them. Judy, Laf, and Ivan Ilych learn necessary lessons that allow them to enlarge their ability to lead lives of their own rather than being completely at the mercy of external accidents. In learning to meet the precondition of alienation, their capacity to live lives of their own is enlarged; they are better able to live their own lives. *They gain greater freedom.* Alienation constricts our lives, it makes it more difficult to live lives of our own, to be the persons we want to be. Alienation deprives us of freedom as John Stuart Mill, writing in the middle of the nineteenth century, defined it: "The only freedom which deserves the name is that of pursuing our own good in our own way, so long as we do not attempt to deprive others of theirs" (Mill 1948:11). Freedom consists of the capacity to live life as one sees fit in order to make it one's own, to direct it in ways one has chosen for oneself. To the extent that one's ability to live a life that makes sense, that is one's own, is limited by one's own incapacities, by lack of recognition by others, and by social conditions that deprive one of the requisite skills, one is alienated and lacks the freedom to seek one's own good one's own way. Lives that make no sense, that do not allow for intelligible choices, or allow only for choices that one can justify by saying "I like it" or "it felt good," are not fully free. When the range of choices is limited to reactions to present stimuli, freedom is extremely narrow, because life is limited to the present moment. There is no room for life projects, for extended stories, for ancestors and children. Only a diminished freedom is available in an impoverished life.

Conceptions of Freedom

Many philosophers, Mill included, give a much more restricted interpretation to this formulation of the concept of freedom. The eighteenth-century political thinkers, such as John Locke in England, regarded government as the main threat to liberty. Governments, they knew, were prone to legislate matters that free citizens should be able to manage themselves. The authorities had been known to establish religions, forcing all citizens to worship a God as defined by a particular clergy. Governments had censored books and pronounced on scientific theories; they had limited the freedom of citizens to travel, to trade, and to dispose of their property as they saw fit. To the political thinkers of the eighteenth century, government power seemed the only impediment to freedom worth considering.

Mill, a century later, realized that the hostility of social groups to those who did not live lives sanctioned by the majority was as serious an obstacle to freedom as the abuse of government power. Intolerance in society and pressures to conform were as inimical to living a free life as government edicts. Even if government did not prescribe religion or ethical norms, social pressure was, in many cases, as effective as the threat of legal sanctions to keep persons from pursuing "our own good in our own way." Mill knew this at firsthand. When still a young man, he met Harriet, wife of Charles Taylor, and they became life companions in the face of severe disapproval from society. Mill lost close friends because his relationship to Mrs. Taylor flew in the face of prevailing morals, and London society at mid-century was not inclined to forgive him.

For Mill, freedom requires a government that protects civil rights and a society that respects the individual's privacy. As long as no one interferes with my pursuit of my own good by violating established rights, or as long as my neighbors don't interfere with what are essentially private matters, I am free to live my life as I please. The government must not legislate religion or ethics. It must not forbid actions that harm no one. My neighbors must allow me to live my life as I please as long as my way of life does not threaten their freedom or security.

Mill gives a very narrow interpretation of his definition of freedom, as if our ability to pursue our own good in our own way were restricted only by the interference of government using its police power to force us to do what we do not want to do, or by society using its power to ostracize for the same ends. This narrow interpretation of freedom still has many advocates (Berlin 1984). But surely freedom may be restricted in many different ways. Many religious schools have left the faithful poorly educated and a prey to superstition, while ecclesiastical institutions used their authority to threaten eternal damnation to those who practiced birth control or ate pork. Religious authority is as effective in restricting freedom as temporal government. In towns where they are the main employer, industries use their power over people's livelihood to extort political and fiscal concessions from the citizens. Disproportionate economic power can be used to make people do something they would rather not do. Government power allows control over information. Misinformed about the evil influences of Jews, or the lack of intelligence of African-Americans, or the threat of disloyalty from Japanese-Americans, people may be misled into treating their neighbors badly. They acquiesce when the government abuses the maligned groups, believing that such evils must be tolerated while their country is in a crisis. The power of the government to distort the truth can be used to seduce citizens into doing what they do not want to do. Official lies limit freedom. The same is true, of course, of lies spread by demagogues or the public relations firms of powerful corporations.

All of these ways of restricting freedom interfere with human lives. The threat of violence, or of hellfire and brimstone, the threat of unemployment, or of a fictitious national disaster, induces people to act contrary to their own values or preferences. Preeminent power of whatever kind curtails liberty. But in addition, freedom is restricted by the very different ranges of opportunity open to different groups. The freedom of populations plagued by poor education, poor nutrition, poor health is more limited than the freedom of groups whose lot is more comfortable. Their efforts to pursue their own good their own way takes place within a much more restricted compass than the choices made by the well fed, well educated, and healthy. It is clear that human beings are constrained not only by the superior power of government, church, or industry but also by the very limited resources offered them in their lives compared to those available to other peoples. Amartya Sen (1999) cites cases of persons forced by poverty to engage in extremely hazardous pursuits. But he also insists that certain economic freedoms are as genuine as political ones and therefore equally part of a good life. Examples are being able to hire yourself out to an employer of your choice rather than being a slave or an indentured servant, or being able to work outside the house—which women, in many parts of the world, are still forbidden to do. One's ability to lead a good life is also restricted by a short life span, which depends not only on the income available but on the availability of social services and health services. Access to a good life is limited in many ways, and we must not focus attention on only some obstacles and neglect the others.[1]

As we begin to reflect about the relation between alienation and freedom, it is very important to stress that general definitions of freedom, like that provided by John Stuart Mill, are capable of a range of quite different interpretations. In our world everyone is on the side of liberty. But very important political differences are concealed below the surface of this agreement. People tend to specify the precise meaning of the word *freedom* in the light of the particular freedoms they miss. The rich and powerful, who have many opportunities and do not fear deprivation or economic dependency, are concerned about possible limitations of their property rights. Accordingly they tend to identify freedom as untrammeled use of their belongings in their own interest (Nozick 1974). For the poor, the despised, and the downtrodden, freedom from want is more important than the freedom to use their property as they please.

External and Internal Constraints

More generous conceptions of freedom, like those of Sen, are nevertheless still incomplete because they only take account of restrictions of freedom that come from the outside, imposed by institutions or by economic and social conditions. All of these conceptions of freedom have to do with limits that are *external* to the agent. But ever since the days of Rousseau in the middle of the eighteenth century, philosophers have wondered whether free citizens do not also need to possess specific personality traits so that they may avail themselves of the freedoms allowed them by society and the government. *Is it self-evident that all human beings will want to or be able to seek their own good their own way, if they are allowed to do so?* If the citizens of a society are to be free, perhaps some conditions *internal* to each person will also have to be met. Freedom is not available to those who do not want to pursue their own good but would rather have someone else tell them what to pursue, or who have some ideas of how they would want to live but are too depressed, too lazy, or too distracted to make any efforts to do so. In a society where living one's own life and being a person in one's own right is not a widely shared goal, freedom is severely limited. In order to be free, one must not only be free of many external interferences; one must also be devoted to being free and be capable of living one's own life. Not everyone is.

The ringing opening of Rousseau's *Social Contract*—"Man is born free and everywhere we see him in chains"—draws our attention to the *internal* requirements for freedom. Rousseau does not merely deplore the ubiquity of tyranny that deprives human beings of their natural-born rights to life and liberty. As the second chapter of the *Social Contract* makes clear, Rousseau thinks of slaves—men and women "in chains"—not as persons forcibly made to work without pay but as persons who "lose everything in their chains, even the desire of escaping from them: they love their servitude as the comrades of Ulysses loved their brutish condition" (Rousseau n.d.:6). He calls "slaves" those persons whose *nature has become servile.* "Everywhere . . . in chains" does not describe societies under the yoke of tyranny but societies whose members have lost the taste for freedom, whose citizens have lost the passion for liberty and an independent sense of who they are. Their lives are not their own; they neither notice nor regret that fact. In societies where all try to please others, where all want to be famous because their self-esteem rests on public acclaim, rather than on pride in living their life as they choose, all lose the ability to be free. Their unfreedom is no longer externally imposed by the powerful but is a result of their own inabilities, of their own needs that only conditions of servitude can satisfy.

A free society requires not only a government that protects rights and liberties and a social structure that allows wide discretion to its citizens in private matters. It also requires citizens intent on using the freedoms available to them and capable of doing so—capable of finding their own path, of sticking to it in the face of opposition from others, of being self-directed. The great theorists of democracy have always been very clear that citizens must be free internally if the institutions that protect their freedoms from constraints by government or fellow citizens are to be effective and permanent. Thomas Jefferson again and again praised farmers as the ideal citizens of a democracy because their life and work fostered in them the character that good citizens need. They are "the most independent, the most virtuous" (Jefferson 1993:351). Artisans, on the other hand, are "the panderers of vice, and the instruments by which the liberties of a country are generally overturned" (p. 351). People who work for wages, who live in cities, who engage in trade and are therefore dependent on the goodwill of their customers, are rendered subservient and venal by that dependence (p. 259). Farmers depend on no one. Their way of life makes them independent persons. They are free not only insofar as they have certain rights but also insofar as they are not constrained by government or society. They are *free persons*—their lives are their own; they are economically independent and therefore able to live by their principles, to pursue their own projects or, in other ways, make their lives intelligible. Life in the city, Jefferson thought, does not encourage that sort of character. City folk, hired help, craftsmen, and people in trade are dependent on others for their living. They get in the habit of catering to others; their circumstances do not encourage them to stand on their own two feet, to think for themselves, and to direct their own lives firmly. But lacking a clear self, they are not well suited to being free citizens. They do not lack freedom from external constraints. They are unfree because they do not think for themselves and are slavishly dependent on the whims and opinions of others. They are constrained not by forces external to them but by their own incapacity for moral rectitude or intellectual independence.

Alexis de Tocqueville, who visited the United States in the 1830s because he so admired American democracy, also recognized the internal constraints on liberty. He believed that the far-going egalitarianism of the United States might well affect the character of citizens adversely:

> The same equality which makes him independent of each separate citizen leaves him isolated and defenseless in the face of the majority. . . . The majority in the United States takes over the business of supplying the individual with a quantity of ready-made opinions and so relieves him of the necessity of forming his own. (de Tocqueville 1988:435)

The rule of the majority, de Tocqueville feared, produces a citizen "overwhelmed by a sense of his insignificance and weakness" (p. 435). Men and women thus rendered unsure of their own persons and identity might well bind themselves "in tight fetters to the general will of the greatest number. . . . [They] would by no means have found the way to live in independence; they would have succeeded in the difficult task of giving slavery a new face" (p. 436). Neither government coercion nor social pressure induces the citizens of a democratic society to "[give] slavery a new face." The unfreedom of these citizens is not externally imposed. Citizens adopt the majority opinion because they are rendered unsure of themselves and what they stand for in the welter of free opinions that overwhelm everyone in a democratic society. Life in a fairly egalitarian society, de Tocqueville thought, weakens the independence of citizens, and that weakness of self may seduce them into conformity and thus make them unfree.

No Freedom for the Alienated

The precise nature of the internal constraints on freedom is not terribly clear in the works of Rousseau, Jefferson, or de Tocqueville. It is difficult to resist the thought that Jefferson's praise of the farmer reflected his own position as landed gentry. Country people are no more independent from the banks, or the buyers of their produce, than city people are from their employers, or customers. But Jefferson did see an important change taking place in America with the rise of capitalism and urbanization, and he rightly feared that the new social order threatened the internal conditions for living one's own life one's own way. Similarly, de Tocqueville's worry about conformism in America is important even though we may doubt the adequacy of his diagnosis of its origins.

With the help of our understanding of the complexities and multiple manifestations of alienation, we can explain in more detail and more plausibly how alienation limits freedom by throwing up internal impediments. External restraints, abuses of overwhelming power, and the absence of basic resources make it more difficult and often impossible for persons to pursue their own good as they would choose were they free to do so. The internal restraints created by alienation make it more difficult to know what one's own good might look like. They also weaken one's capacities to pursue that good once it has been identified. This is more easily understood against the background of some actual examples of alienation.

Examples of Alienation

On August 31, 1997, Princess Diana was killed in an automobile accident. Thousands of people felt terribly bereaved and mourned deeply for her, bringing flowers to the square in front of Kensington Palace with messages expressing their love for the dead princess and their certainty that she had loved them, even though they had never met. They had known about her only from the tabloids and from television. It is difficult to resist the sense that, however heartfelt these emotions, they were not quite real, but expressed the fantasies of people for whom the love in their lives was not sufficient. Romantic love, passionate and engrossing, tries to escape an actual world that is unsatisfying. How much more is this passion, when directed at persons unknown, a reflection of lives felt to be lacking, to be drab, and boring? Loved by the glamorous princess, I am touched by her splendor; I am, at least for a short while, a more valuable and important person than the world has led me to believe.

Alienation has something to do with the response to Diana's death, with the romantic fantasies that swirled around the dead princess. Besides, the public felt that the princess had been treated shabbily by the Royal Family and was being snubbed even in death. Resentment is a common feeling among the alienated—resentment at feeling so powerless, at lives that seem irremediably pointless. Diana's death provided an outlet for that widespread resentment.

Alienated lives are boring and any escape from tedium is welcome. For many, no doubt, it was the excitement and the interruption of everyday routines that attracted them to the long lines to sign their name in the memorial book, or to join the vigil outside Kensington Palace. Alienated lives are always in search of novelty. An ominous example of that comes from Peter Handke's memoir about his mother's life in Germany and Austria. In 1938, when the Nazis took over Austria,

"We were kind of excited," my mother told me. For the first time, people did things together. Even the daily grind took on a festive mood. . . . For once, everything that was strange and incomprehensible in the world took on meaning and became part of a larger context. . . . She still had no interest in politics; what was happening before her eyes was something entirely different from politics. (Handke 1974:14)

Meaningless lives—"everything that was strange and incomprehensible"—suddenly seemed to gain a new significance with the excitement over the Nazi annexation of Austria. For a brief period it looked as if life might be intelligible after all; never mind that the real, political import of the events was not understood. Life's new meaning was unconnected to real events; it was meaning based in fantasy, in the excitement of flag-waving crowds, in the faint promise of a change not only in politics but in life as a whole. The political change portended a new world, a world of possibilities and fulfillment that had not existed before. People did things together, the isolation and strangling loneliness that are part of alienation seemed overcome; a new feeling of community replaced the dull depression of being alone. Needless to say, that community soon collapsed because it had been imaginary all along.

When real selves are scarce, we adopt fantasy selves; when real life is dreary, we escape into fantasy life. When Princess Diana died, fantasy life, fantasy love, abetted by the media, took precedence over feelings for real persons to whom one had real ties. People who did not know Princess

Diana were sure that she loved them, and they discovered that they loved her also. But what sort of love is it that has an unknown as its object? Can it be real? Who were they really weeping for? One of the mourners for Princess Diana said that "he cried more at Diana's funeral than at his father's eight years earlier" (Merck 1998:27). Mourning for a real person, especially a parent, carries some danger with it. The loss is deep. Will one be able to stem the flood of tears once they are allowed to come? With grief one may also open oneself to anger, disappointment, and the animosity one feels toward parents—emotions that are thoroughly frightening. Real relations are beset by ambivalence; they are confusing. It requires a firm self, confidence in oneself and the confidence that comfort can be had when one needs it, to let oneself sorrow over the death of a father. All of this is difficult for the alienated, whose sense of themselves is beset by self-doubt. What a release, therefore, to be able to grieve openly about an unknown, a person who was as one imagines her. One can feel grief safely here because no ambivalence corrodes one's love. What is more, whereas one's father's death was much more private and therefore one's grief more readily embarrassing, here grief is shared; one need not be ashamed in front of others. The alienated worry a great deal about what others think of them. But they did not have to worry about that in front of Kensington Palace. There the isolated found a sudden community—albeit with perfect strangers—so seductive to those who feel terribly alone. For once they were not competitors; they were not distanced from each other by trying to appear as someone they were not. No one was trying to impress anyone else. In the emotion of the moment, they felt more free because less oppressed by the fear of looking silly, of being laughed at, of being disliked or bullied.

Without self-confidence, being a person in one's own right is very frightening. What if no one will like the person I become? What if I invite ridicule and ostracism? Easier to allow the fashion authorities to choose for me who I am to be. Hence people look to commercial forces to determine today's "look," to decide who they are.

> "Right now I'm in the middle of a style change. I am making myself miserable as I wait for my hair to grow out from an extremely short, close-shaven cut. That haircut was my favorite. It was easy to care for. It looked great. I was always complimented . . . so why change it? The androgynous, short-haired look of Annie Lenox has been replaced by the more feminine locks of Pauline Prizkova. Her image is everywhere nowadays. It is her image that is making me desire longer hair. So I will add that to me." (quoted in Ewen 1988:20–21)

The shaping of identities is given over to the dress designers, the producers of beauty products, of hair fashions. Identity itself becomes a commodity.

The self-esteem of the alienated rises when they see themselves on television. Being watched by strangers is as close as they can come to the affectionate regard of family and friends to help them construct their identity. People get a lot of respect and attention not for being who they are but for being a "celebrity," because they were on *Donahue*. Gay men who are accustomed to physical violence in public are no longer threatened by straight men once they are recognized as the gay couple that was on *Oprah*. "Many noted that they were more popular with friends and associates after their appearances [on a TV talk show]" (Priest 1996). Having been chosen by a producer to appear on a television show gives one a seal of approval. The tyranny of appearances is manifest when one's worth is fixed by appearing before a very large television audience. Being seen by millions, if only for a brief moment, gives one respectability. It is no longer of importance how I conduct myself in relation to other persons; my legitimacy derives from being watched by large numbers of anonymous viewers. Being known to my neighbors or to the townspeople is not as good because there are so few of them. It is the size of the audience that has looked at me that certifies me as a person of substance. No longer individuals in our own right and our own persons, we gain reality only in the gaze of the public. Television and its producers become the arbiters for who is a worthwhile person. The alienated do not trust their own judgment and cannot pick their own heroes. Television helps by telling them whom to admire. The alienated do not even know whether to respect themselves and they trust television to tell them that, too. Once one has appeared on the television screen, one can feel more confident of one's worth.

A Serious Objection

I seem to be pointing at the lives of others and labeling them defective. That realization brings me up short. Who are you, I say to myself, to judge the lives of others, to determine who is oneself and who lacks a firm self and whose life makes sense? No, I would probably not have spent long days and nights in the vigil for Princess Diana. I do not change my appearance periodically to conform to the latest images promoted by men's fashion magazines. But what is wrong with mourning the sudden death of a popular personage, or trying to be as chic as possible, or, like Peter Handke's mother, even feeling a flutter of hope with all the political changes, the flags, the parades—hope for a life less oppressed than hers had been so far? People are different, they lead different lives, and no one is entitled to condemn other lives just because they are different from one's own. Why condemn the life sought by all in Emma Bovary's country town? What is wrong with wanting to be rich? To be famous? To appear better than one is?

This objection can take different forms. In one, the objection assumes that there is no intelligible reason for preferring one way of life over another. People live the way they live and who is to say that one person's life is better than another? Such complete agnosticism as to the relative value of different lives is unacceptable. When I am in despair because my life has come to a dead end and is unbearably monotonous, I do not want to be told that one life is as good as another and that one cannot judge one to be better than another. I know that my life is terrible and that other people live better lives. Some lives are better than others, and even though our assessments are open to controversy and agreement is sometimes impossible to reach, it is legitimate to compare lives and express a preference for one over another.

In another form, the objection constitutes a needed reminder that it is difficult to pass reliable judgments on the lives of others, unless we are very intimately acquainted with them. Even someone we know rather well, whose life we envy because it seems filled with exciting events and significant accomplishments, may surprise us by confessing that he is bored, discouraged, and feels inadequate. It is difficult to be certain about the form alienation takes in the life of others. Even one's judgments about the effects of alienation in one's own life are not infallible. One should speak of alienation with caution and humility.

In a third form, the objection insists that we must be careful not to use the jargon of alienation to cloak our own prejudices and to proclaim our lives more perfect than those of others. Intellectuals do not always resist the temptation to use what understanding we have of alienation to try to make ourselves feel better by pointing to the barren lives of others. We fulminate against the conformism of others, snicker at the foolish consumers of mass entertainment, and show contempt for rampant commercialism. We exempt ourselves from the problems of alienation and treat them as an indication of the worthlessness of the rest of humanity. But intellectuals are as subject to fashions in their work, in the jargon they use, and in the attitude they strike as anyone else. They misuse the idea of alienation when they use it to criticize the rest of humanity. It is not the purpose of discussions of alienation to humiliate others and to build oneself up. Rather, their aim is to bring to light the problems that the precondition of alienation raises for us all, including the intellectuals, and to explore how some societies restrict more seriously than others the possibility of resisting the precondition of alienation.

Alienation is not the result of moral failings or defective character. Different persons find themselves in different conditions; sometimes their lives can gain some intelligibility, sometimes not. Some lives are more clearly one's own; some persons have a recognizable identity, others do not. In speaking about specific instances of alienation we do not blame the persons involved but, rather, acknowledge that life has dealt them a poor hand, that they did not have the opportunities to acquire the knowledge and skills needed to make some sense out of *their* life, the life that they found themselves living when they first reached adulthood. The target of the theory of alienation is society, which makes it very difficult to lead lives that cohere and make some sense, and defeats efforts to be oneself with a clear identity. Alienation restricts the alternatives open to all of us; we have limited freedom.

The Difficulty of Choosing One's Own Good

Philosophers tend to imagine that one chooses one's own good by formulating a life plan. Persons who have their life mapped out in general are pursuing their own good. But Ivan Ilych's history shows the poverty of that conception. Yes, to be sure, Ivan Ilych had a life plan, but his plan was precisely not to venture to be his own person, or to live the life that was specifically his own. His plan was, on the contrary, to fit in, to be conformist and make no waves. The alienated, those who are too timid or perhaps too indolent to seek firm identities of their own, can very well make their own life plans.

The young person who chooses to be a doctor, a lawyer, a professor has not thereby formed a distinct identity. His first discovery will be that there may well be different ways of being a doctor, a lawyer, or a professor. It will take him much longer to discover in what particular way he wants to follow his chosen occupation. Perhaps the teacher discovers talents for being a brilliant lecturer but, in small groups, finds herself tongue-tied and at a loss to understand the students. But, of course, the lecturer has many further choices to make in determining what kind of teacher she is going to be. Finding one's own good is a very extended process; one discovers one's own good by getting to know oneself, one's abilities and preferences, and various alternatives the world has to offer.

For many persons, the choice of work is not as inspiring as it is for professionals. Most work is fairly humdrum and the position of the worker more or
less humiliating. But even here, choices important to the definition of the self
must be made. Many kinds of work allow the employee to cheat the employer, by dipping in the till, by taking tools home from work, by doing private e-mail when one is supposed to be doing the boss's work. In any work
situation, moral choices present themselves. There are choices about the extent to which one knuckles under to the employer's demands. Employers like
their workers to buy the goods and brands they produce, or to communicate
with customers in set ways. Relations in the workplace constantly challenge
one's autonomy and self-assertion. These choices have a direct effect on the
extent to which one is one's own person and has a clear identity.

In the course of self-discovery—of discovering what one can do well,
what one likes, and what is acceptable—it is of the essence that one be able
to recognize when problems arise. One of the great challenges in human
lives is to recognize problems. Some crises are undeniable: There's no food
in the house; the rent is due and we have no money; I need to go to work
and the car won't start. But many other difficulties begin much more subtly. Something does not feel quite right but, to begin with, it's not clear
what this something is or what about it is not right. One can meet such
faint incipient discomforts in very different ways. I can say "Oh, it's nothing" and turn on the TV, or take a drink. Or I can say "I wonder what's going on" and decide to keep an eye on this discomfort in order to make
sure that it is not just a momentary sadness wafting across one's life. If the
sense of discomfort continues, and it becomes clear that an important relationship, for instance, is unfulfilling, or contentious, I can tell myself not to
be silly, or blame myself for being irritable, or unsupportive, taking the
onus on myself and thereby turning my back on the problem. I can ask
myself whether my complaints merely reflect my own state. Am I depressed, am I sick, am I aging and feeling despair over my waning powers?
Or is this relation really lacking in energy? Have we become distracted
from each other, or have we changed? Have we failed to pay attention
where attention was needed? Perhaps there is a difficulty in the relationship and it needs to be faced. Or if something in my work seems not to be
right, I can ignore it, but I can also take the feeling seriously and try to understand it better. Is there something seriously amiss with the work? Am I
not doing it in a way that fits my nature?

Before he fell ill, Ivan Ilych encountered a situation like that. His work
seemed no longer right, he was distracted, felt out of sorts, and was irritable and unhappy. When he took an extended vacation and went to live in

the country, he was incredibly restless and felt at loose ends. He did what everyone else would do in this situation: He drew on the accepted wisdom of the society and diagnosed his unhappiness as due to lack of money. Once that was decided, he busied himself and secured a better job. Soon after the move to the new job, he fell ill and discovered that it was not lack of money that was behind his previous unease but the very much more serious failure of his life to be anchored in strong human relations. He lacked the sense that he was living his own life and instead was forever trying to please everyone else.

Making a life for oneself often does not consist of making explicit choices to live in this way or that but, rather, involves recognizing the signs that changes may be needed, that one's life is not going as well as one would like, or that an opportunity is opening up for making it more one's own. Those signs are easily missed altogether or misinterpreted. The example involving Ivan Ilych also shows how choosing one's own good and pursuing it are part of one and the same process. One must learn to take one's own perceptions seriously, but the temptation, of course, is to diagnose those perceptions according to prevailing opinion. It is only by acting on one's choices that one discovers whether one is indeed pursuing one's own good or perhaps has accepted bad advice and gone in the wrong direction. When situations do not feel right, the uneasiness is vague and needs to be diagnosed. At first, of course, one will draw on prevailing opinion in giving those diagnoses; then one will test them in action. If one misapplies the prevailing opinion, or if that opinion is unreliable, the actions that follow will not cure one's malaise.

One discovers one's own good in the pursuit of it. It is a process of experimentation in the course of which one discovers one's self and becomes one's own person to some extent. We rarely make up our own prescriptions for the difficulties we encounter in the course of finding our own good but, instead, rely on the common wisdom in our social environment. Ivan Ilych's experience illustrates one way in which capitalism misleads us. The society in which we live incessantly counsels us to solve our problems by spending money, and thus suggests that if we do have difficulties, more money will probably solve them. If your work no longer satisfies, take a job that pays more. If your family life is unsatisfactory, get a more expensive therapist, or buy a bigger house, or a fancier car. As we have seen, capitalism encourages us to think about and treat ourselves exclusively as economic agents, motivated by nothing so much as the inclination to "truck and barter." But as economic agents we are not concerned about the meaning of our lives, about their continuity, or whether they are our own in any sense. As economic agents we try to profit from accidents or reduce the losses they inflict on us, but we do not ask how a life propelled by accidental happenings can nevertheless be meaningful and our own. In this way, too, capitalism encourages alienation by deflecting attention from the meaning and coherence of one's own life.

To the extent that meaning and coherence do matter, finding one's own good involves one in a process of discovery, of experimentation, of retracing one's steps if a problem was misdiagnosed and setting out in a different direction. Such a process involves risks, of failure, of making bad choices, of getting lost. One may have to brave the criticism of friends and neighbors and bear the disapproval of those who do not understand. In order to pursue one's own good, one must take oneself seriously. (Taking oneself seriously does not mean that one takes all of one's emotions at face value and acts on every complaint. There is a difference between complaining incessantly or being terribly demanding and taking oneself seriously. There is also an important difference between being excessively self-involved and self-centered and taking oneself seriously.) For the alienated, unsure of themselves, distrusting their own sensibilities and their own judgments, fearful of change, the temptation is to ignore this faint discomfort. Perhaps a change of scene, a trip to the amusement park, a quick love affair will fix everything. Discomforts may be discounted as soon as they are felt. The alienated, whose selves are diffuse, do not know which emotions of theirs to trust and which to overlook. Either they take none of their feeling seriously, perhaps criticizing themselves for being ungrateful for the good they do have, or they are unable to distinguish between a passing discomfort and a feeling manifesting a more serious fissure.

Similar challenges rise up when there seems to be something missing. I have no complaints about my work, or about my friends, but somewhere, in the back of my mind, there is a persistent voice that asks: Is that all there is? I can evade this difficulty by chiding myself for being too demanding. I can exhort myself to be "realistic" and tell myself that once we reach middle age, there is less excitement in life than in the earlier years. But I can also take this empty feeling more seriously. I need not immediately change my job, or my friends, or look for some adventure that is, for me, totally unsuitable, but I can watch and wait. I can reflect about my life; I can talk to my friends and if a course of Saint Johns Wort turns out not to help, perhaps I need to examine my life more carefully.

Taking oneself seriously includes being willing to change, if that seems to be necessary. But change, in many situations, is frightening. It is not easy to give up what one has now for an unknown situation that may not be better. Before changing partners, changing one's job, making new friends, or taking up a new hobby, one wants to make sure that the changes will bring improvements. One wants to be reasonably sure that the new undertakings will not end in complete disaster and leave one worse off than before. Being serious about oneself and one's life requires courage.

At the same time, if one takes oneself seriously, one is willing to wait. One understands that life is only marginally under our control. A better life is not available to us the moment we wish for it; one needs to be patient and wait for the right opportunity to make improvements. One also understands that our lives are not transparent to us. Our emotions and perceptions are fragmentary communications in a language we do not always understand. There is a message in our feeling out of sorts in a relationship or being disinterested in much of our present life, but that message is not easily deciphered. If one panics or ignores these messages, life may well go on but it will be less one's own. The signs and portents of one's own emotions need to be attended to carefully, but it takes patience to wait until we learn to understand them.

Persons in possession of themselves, finally, are ready to act. Being a reasonably definite person, one does what is appropriate to one's personality when the occasion calls for it. Alienation manifests itself in endless indecision, or in retrospective worrying about what one did but should not have done, about opportunities missed, about the cutting retort that would have restored one's upper hand in a conflict. Sometimes one needs to wait patiently until a problem clarifies itself or a long-awaited opportunity presents itself. At other times one just acts.

In these many different ways, choosing one's own good is a deliberate, extended process. It requires, first of all, considerable confidence in oneself. One needs to trust one's perceptions and be clear about what one understands and what one doesn't. One needs to take oneself seriously by not belittling or denying one's own discomforts or hopes. If changes need to be made or are forced upon one by circumstances, one needs a certain amount of confidence in one's own ability to improvise, to change, and to invent ways of maintaining one's identity under different conditions. One must trust that one is not totally misguided, one must trust one's perceptions of what is important so that one can try to pursue those important values even when that is difficult or requires sacrifices. Equally important, one must also trust others to help if help is needed, to give one the respect one deserves, not to take advantage of one's weakness, and to allow one the space one needs to shape one's own identity. One gains that sort of self-confidence, sureness, and trust in oneself and others if one participates in group life and group projects where one's identity, in all its uniqueness, is acknowledged and appreciated. (See the section titled "Recognition" in Chapter 3.)

Alienation leaves us with insufficient self-confidence, with a faint sense of our own powers or of who we are. It makes it difficult for us to trust in our own strengths or in the goodwill and affection of others. If we are reduced to finding instant community in large media-inspired events like the public mourning for Princess Diana, if we are so little confident in our own person that we need to change our "image" when fashions change, if we trust so little in our own judgment that we must wait for television to make us into significant persons, then developing a firmer self in the ways sketched out above is very difficult.

Being alienated, one cannot pursue one's own good in one's own way, because one is unable to gain a clear sense of what one's own good might possibly be, and one is too timid, too distrustful of oneself and one's own impulses to pursue a good even if one has a glimpse of it. The alienated lack the self-confidence for considering their own discomforts; they are too frightened to contemplate change unless it is imposed on them by unintelligible accidents; they do not value themselves sufficiently to take risks for the sake of maintaining that self when the world around them changes radically. In all these ways, they are unable to have lives of their own. They cannot make something of what is given to them or tell an intelligible story about the jumbled events of their lives. Incomprehension, timidity, indecisiveness, passivity, fearfulness, self-distrust and distrust of others, thinly disguised resentment about their own impotence, endless longing for love, community, and excitement restrict their choices on all sides. Their lives are barely their own. Alienation is the enemy of freedom.[2]

Capitalism and Political Freedom

Alienation imposes serious internal constraints on freedom. But does it also affect the external constraints imposed by governments or by oppressive majorities? Capitalism is often thought to be a necessary condition for external freedoms or, if not a necessary condition, at least an important facilitating factor (Friedman and Friedman 1962). Civil liberties and restrictions on government power came into the world during the same historical period in which the capitalist system developed in England and, later, in Western Europe. Those two historical developments were mutually supportive of each other. An economic system that encourages individual commercial initiative may well look favorably on a limitation of government power. Citizens who desire greater individual freedom may well feel comfortable in an economic system that allows them to strike out for themselves in directions they themselves have chosen.

So it may appear, at first, that although alienation weakens our ability to be persons in our own right because it makes us more dependent on public approval and the vagaries of fashion, the civil and political liberties that are integral to a democratic society are not affected by the alienation that capitalism fosters. We can still be free citizens, however impaired our ability is to make sense of our own lives. But the matter is not quite that simple. Actually functioning democratic institutions are complex systems. At one level are the legal foundations, some written out in constitutions, others simply traditions followed for many years. Then there are various judicial, legislative, executive institutions that wield power, make rules, review troublesome disputes. Constitutions and functioning institutions are surrounded by a welter of practices and informal groupings. There are political parties, neighborhood political committees, ad hoc organizations to get someone elected, groups formed to present a particular problem to the elected representatives. Less formal are the public discussions in workplaces, bar rooms, and barbershops.

This systemic complexity allows democratic institutions to exist in very different conditions. At one extreme is a vibrant democracy with widespread popular participation that attracts keen interest on all sides, stimulating discussion and serious reflection about the problems of the day as well as about long-term concerns over the structure of existing institutions. De Tocqueville's description of American democracy in the 1830s presents a good example of such a lively democracy:

> No sooner do you set forth on American soil than you find yourself in a sort of tumult. . . . All-around everything is on the move: here the people of a district are assembled to discuss the possibility of building a church; there they are busy choosing a representative; further on, the delegates of a district are hurrying to town to consult about some local improvements; elsewhere it's the village farmers who have left their furrows to discuss the plan for a road or school. . . . It is hard to explain the place filled by political concerns in the life of an American. To take a hand in the government of society and to talk about it is his most important business and, so to say, the only pleasure he knows. That is obvious even in the most trivial habits of his life; even the women often go to public meetings and forget household cares while they listen to political speeches. For them clubs to some extent takes the place of theaters. (de Tocqueville 1969:242–243)

At the other extreme is a country that has a democratic constitution and all the requisite governmental functions, but the government is not effectively supervised or instructed by the citizenry because they lose interest or find the political process too time-consuming or too frustrating when their wishes are not met immediately. Democratic institutions function only minimally or not at all. Such a country is democratic in name only. This is more like American democracy today, where less than half the people vote, few are well informed about the affairs of their nation, and many care more for sports than for politics. Alienation encourages distrust. People do not trust their government; they believe, not without reason, that it is largely run by the wealthy and by large corporations. Despair and a sense of powerlessness, hallmarks of alienation, discourage political activity. Citizens withdraw and their only form of participation is carping criticism. The institutions of government and industry are no longer in the service of the people. Unlike the government of Americans in the 1830s, today's government is no longer ours in any real sense.

Any society requires the elaborate machinery of democracy that protects citizens against abuse of government power and oppression from social groups. Without such protections, citizens will find themselves sooner or later constrained by ruthless governors pursuing power and wealth, or by fanatical social groups who, convinced of the absolute rightness of their own beliefs, are completely intolerant of different opinions. Freedom, even in a well-functioning democratic society, is always precarious. Defenses against oppression must constantly be reinforced in order to keep the democratic machinery running smoothly and effectively. There is no nation that can preserve its freedom without vigorous struggle in its defense.

Here the effect of alienation on democratic institutions makes itself felt. To the extent that citizens in capitalist countries are conformists rather than seeking lives of their own—to the extent that they are indecisive, filled with self-distrust, unclear about what matters to them, isolated, and prepared to give the management of their lives over to mass media, to government agencies such as the military, or to religious authorities—they are less able and less likely to defend their freedoms, political and civil, when they appear to be under attack. As soon as their security seems threatened, they acquiesce in government attempts to limit their freedoms. For persons who make few serious choices on their own, who have no opinions of their own, freedom is second in importance to comfort and security, to traveling with ease, to being entertained in their homes. Alienated citizens are not going to be persistent defenders of their freedoms. Freedoms not defended will be hollowed out: The forms of democracy will remain, but their substance will slowly be eroded from the inside.

In this way alienation weakens not only internal freedom—the freedom to be a person in one's own right—but also the more familiar political and civil liberties that are at the heart of a functioning democracy.

Conclusion

In the world of alienation, appearances are supreme, deception is rampant, and it behooves one to be very distrustful. Alienation itself is denied; the forms of freedom prevail but freedom itself loses strength everyday. The language of setting goals for oneself, of "being all one can be," of "seeking one's own good in one's own way," is still in use, but the words have been drained of meaning; they are no longer taken seriously. In truth, most people think that these phrases refer to getting rich and consuming mightily. Behind the affluent façade of our society hide persons unsure of themselves, dependent upon the latest experts for advice on how to be happy, how to find satisfactory relationships, and how to raise their children. A great deal of money is being made by giving bad advice to people who cannot trust themselves anymore. The right to speak publicly and to be heard goes to the rich, and they hire as their writers men and women who will offend the fewest readers. The marketplace incessantly pushes us all to consume mass-produced goods such as cars, houses, and clothing, and just as many mass-produced reflections about the good life. We have learned to commodify ourselves. If all that leaves us dissatisfied because something important seems to be missing and important goals seem to have escaped us, few of us are able to value ourselves sufficiently to listen to these inner complaints seriously, and fewer still are able even to think about what might be the matter.

No wonder that we live in a world more affluent and less happy than ever—bewildered, frightened, and adrift, we turn away from our work as citizens as defenders of our freedoms. We have become incapable of finding community because we cannot trust anyone. We turn our backs on our neighbors' suffering—so grim are our own lives that we cannot bear to feel the pain of others. We fall into addictions, overwork, violence—physical or verbal. We respond to fear of death by renewing our health club memberships. Our world has become very small; only the immediate family, and perhaps, work are of interest to us. What happens to other people in other countries does not concern us. Life has become a spectacle that we watch bemused and dissatisfied. Our much-vaunted civilization has become a sorry affair, a theatrical performance in which we don't know our lines but must wait for the prompter—most likely a pundit in the pay of Disney or some other multinational corporation—to feed us spurious pieces of wisdom.

We can continue this downward path toward a society ever more regimented, manipulated, and self-deceived, or we can band together with groups of friends and, looking away from our own comfort and convenience, face the poverty, cruelty, and tyranny that dominate the world. In bestirring ourselves to heal the world, we reassert our humanity and reclaim our lives for ourselves. Protesting our own commodification, we can affirm once again the humanity of each of us—that human beings are ends in themselves and should not be treated as means to the ends of power-hungry governments or corporations seeking fatter profits. We must set our faces against the coldhearted cost-benefit calculations with respect to human lives and human deprivation. Jointly with others we can expand our powers and transform the commodified world once again into a human world by reclaiming it from the manipulators in boardrooms, from the violent men who drown the world in blood, from the plans made for us by experts. In protesting, resisting, and acting we will once again make our freedoms count by asserting them forcefully and revive our democracy as the rule of all of us—the people—and not only of the rich and their public relations firms and lobbyists. Turning our backs on the seductive comforts and narcotizing conveniences of the world of commodities, we shall try to build a free society where each furthers his or her own well-being and promotes that of the others.

Notes

1. John Rawls counters this observation by distinguishing between freedom and the worth of freedom. We could then say that students who come to school hungry, whose teacher is ignorant, are as free to get an education as students attending the most elite institution—except that the freedom of the poor students is not worth a lot (Rawls 1971:204). But that distinction is sophistical. If Joe drives a fancy car and Bill's car rarely starts, shall we say they are both mobile but Bill's mobility is worth less? If Sue and Ellen both have pockets full of money, shall we say they are both rich even though Sue's bills are a worthless currency? The fact that oppression has many faces cannot be erased by making a distinction.

2. I have tried to work out some of these ideas about the hindrance that alienation is to freedom in my essay "Socialist Freedom" in Anatol Anton and Richard Schmitt, eds., *Socialism for a New Generation* (forthcoming).

References

Anton, Anatole, Milton Fisk, and Nancy Holmstrom, eds. (2000). *Not for Sale: In Defense of Public Goods*. Boulder: Westview Press.

Anzaldúa, Gloria (1987). *La Frontera/Borderlands: The New Mestiza*. San Francisco: Spinster/aunt lute.

Arnold, N. Scott (1990). *Marx's Radical Critique of Capitalist Society: A Reconstruction and Critical Evaluation*. Oxford: Oxford University Press.

Baldwin, James (1963). *The Fire Next Time*. New York: Dial.

Barker, Pat (1995). *The Eye in the Door*. New York: Penguin.

Bartky, Sandra Lee (1990). "On Psychological Oppression." In *Feminity and Domination*. New York: Routledge.

Becker, Gary (1986). "The Economic Approach to Human Behavior." In *Rational Choice*, ed. Jon Elster. New York: New York University Press.

Benn, S. I. (1975–1976). "Freedom, Autonomy, and the Concept of a Person." *Proceedings Aristotelian Society NS [New Series]* 76:109–130.

Berlin, Isaiah (1984). "Two Concepts of Liberty." In *Liberalism and Its Critics*, ed. Michael Sandel. Oxford: Oxford University Press.

Bowles, Samuel (1998). "Endogenous Preferences: The Cultural Consequences of Markets and Other Institutions." *Journal of Economic Literature* 36:75–111.

Brison, Susan J. (1997). "Outliving Oneself: Trauma, Memory and Personal Identity." In *Feminists Rethink the Self*, ed. Diana Tietjens Meyers. Boulder: Westview Press.

Davion, V. (1987). "Do Good Feminists Compete?" *Hypatia* 2:55–63.

de Graaf, John, David Wann, and Thomas H. Naylor (2001). *Affluenza: The All-Consuming Epidemic*. San Francisco: Barrett-Kohler Publishers.

Deming, Barbara (1984). *We Are All Part of One Another: A Barbara Deming Reader*, ed. Jane Meyerding. Philadelphia: New Society Publishers.

de Tocqueville, Alexis (1988). *Democracy in America*. New York: Harper Perennial.

Dickens, Charles (2000). *A Tale of Two Cities*. London: Penguin.

Dostoyevsky, Fyodor. (n.d.). *Notes from the Underground*. New York: Modern Library.

Dufresne, John (1997). *Love Warps the Mind a Little.* New York: Plume.

Eliot, T. S. (1963). *Collected Poems, 1909–1962.* London: Faber & Faber.

Ende, Michael (1974). *Momo.* Harmondsworth: Penguin.

Ewen, Stuart (1988). *All-Consuming Images: The Politics of Style in Contemporary Culture.* New York: Basic Books.

Flaubert, Gustave (1989). *Madame Bovary.* New York: Bantam.

Frankl, Viktor E. (1974). *Man's Search for Meaning.* New York: Pocketbooks.

Friedan, Betty (1964). *The Feminine Mystique.* New York: Norton.

Friedman, Milton, and Rose Friedman (1962). *Capitalism and Freedom.* New York: Vintage Books.

Galeano, Eduardo (1998). *Patas Arriba: La Escuela del Mundo al Reves.* Mexico: Siglo XXI.

Grenier, Guillermo (1988). *Inhuman Relations: Quality Circles and Anti-Unionism in American Industry.* Philadelphia: Temple University Press.

Handke, Peter (1974). *A Sorrow Beyond Dreams.* New York: Farrar, Straus and Giroux.

Heidegger, Martin (1929). *Sein und Zeit.* Tuebingen: Max Niemeyer.

Holmstrom, Nancy (2000). "Rationality, Solidarity, and Public Goods." In *In Defense of Public Goods*, ed. Anatole Anton, Milton Fisk, and Nancy Holmstrom. Boulder: Westview Press.

Jefferson, Thomas (1993). *The Life and Selected Writings of Thomas Jefferson,* ed. Adrienne Koch and William Peden. New York: Random House.

Kafka, Franz (1952). *Selected Short Stories of Franz Kafka.* New York: Modern Library.

Kateb, George (1989). "Democratic Individuality and the Meaning of Rights." In *Liberalism and the Moral Life*, ed. Nancy L. Rosenblum. Cambridge: Harvard University Press.

Kenworthy, Lane (1990). "What Kind of Economic System: A Leftist Guide." *Socialist Review* 20:102–123.

Kierkegaard, Søren. (1941a). *Concluding Unscientific Postscript.* Princeton: Princeton University Press.

——— (1941b). *Sickness unto Death.* Princeton: Princeton University Press.

——— (1959). *Either/Or* (Vols. I and II). Princeton: Princeton University Press.

——— (1962). *The Point of View for My Work as an Author: A Report to History.* New York: Harper Torchbooks.

King, Martin Luther, Jr. (1963). *Strength to Love.* Philadelphia: Fortress Press.

Klemke, E. D., ed. (1981). *The Meaning of Life.* New York: Oxford University Press.

Knight, Frank H. (1935). *The Ethics of Competition and Other Essays.* New York: Harper and Brothers.

Kohut, Heinz (1977). *The Restoration of the Self.* New York: International University Press.

Krimerman, Len, and Frank Lindenfeld (1992). *When Workers Decide: Workplace Democracy Takes Root in North America.* Philadelphia: New Society Publishers.

Lane, Robert E. (2000). *The Loss of Happiness in Market Democracies.* New Haven: Yale University Press.

Lasch, Christopher (1978). *The Culture of Narcissism: American Life in an Age of Diminishing Expectations.* New York: Norton.

———— (1984). *The Minimal Self: Psychic Survival in Troubled Times.* New York: Norton.

Longino, Helen E. (1987). "The Ideology of Competition." In *Competition: A Feminist Taboo?* ed. Valerie Miner and Helen E. Longino. New York: The Feminist Press.

Luntley, Michael (1989). *The Meaning of Socialism.* La Salle: Open Court.

Marx, Karl (1867). *Capital* (Vol. I). New York: International Publishers.

———— (1963). *Karl Marx: Early Writings,* ed. T. B. Bottomore. New York: Mc-Graw-Hill.

McMurtry, John (1991). "How Competition Goes Wrong." *Journal of Applied Philosophy* 8:201–209.

Merck, Mandy (1998). *After Diana: Irreverent Elegies.* London: Verso.

Mill, John Stuart (1948). *On Liberty and Considerations on Representative Government.* Oxford: Blackwell.

———— (1949). *Utilitarianism,* ed. John P. Plamenatz. Oxford: Blackwell.

Nietzsche, Friedrich (1954). "Thus Spoke Zarathustra." In *The Portable Nietzsche,* ed. Walter Kaufman. New York: Penguin.

———— (1968). *The Will to Power.* New York: Vintage.

———— (1969). *The Genealogy of Morals.* New York: Vintage Books.

Noddings, Nel (1984). *Caring—A Feminine Approach to Ethics and Moral Education.* Berkeley: University of California Press.

Nozick, Robert (1974). *Anarchy State and Utopia.* New York: Basic Books.

Nussbaum, Martha (1999). *Sex and Social Justice.* New York: Oxford University Press.

Peffer, R. G. (1990). *Marxism, Morality and Social Justice.* Princeton: Princeton University Press.

Percy, Walker (1998). *The Moviegoer.* New York: Vintage International.

Posner, Richard (1992). *Economic Analysis of Law.* Boston: Little, Brown.

Popitz, Heinrich (1968). *Der Entfremdete Mensch: Zeitkritik und Geschichtsphilosophie des jungen Marx.* Frankfurt/Main: Europaeische Verlagsanstalt.

Pratt, Minnie Bruce (1984). "Identity: Skin Blood Heart." In *Yours in Struggle: Three Feminist Perspectives on Anti-Semitism and Racism,* ed. Ellie Bulkin. New York: Long Haul Press.

Priest, Patricia J. (1996). "Gilt by Association": Talk Show Participants' Televisually Enhanced Status and Self-Esteem." In *Constructing the Self in a Mediated World*, ed. Debra Grodin and Thomas R. Lindlof. Thousand Oaks: Sage.

Putnam, Robert (1995). "Bowling Alone." *Journal of Democracy* 6:65–78.

Radin, Margaret J. (1996). *Contested Commodities.* Cambridge: Harvard University Press.

Rawls, John (1971). *A Theory of Justice.* Cambridge: Harvard University Press.

Roemer, John (1994). *A Future for Socialism.* Cambridge: Harvard University Press.

Rousseau, Jean-Jaques (1950). *Discourse on the Origin and Foundation of the Inequality of Mankind.* New York: E. P. Dutton and Company.

———— (1986). *Discourse on the Sciences and the Arts.* In *The First and Second Discourses*, ed. Victor Gourevich. New York: Harper and Row.

———— (1990). *Rousseau, Judge of Jean-Jaques.* Hanover: University Press of New England.

———— (1993). *Emile.* London: Everyman.

———— (n.d.). *The Social Contract.* New York: Dutton.

Rowling, J. K. (1998). *Harry Potter and the Sorcerer's Stone.* New York: Scholastic, Inc.

Sartre, Jean-Paul (1964). *Nausea.* New York: New Directions.

Schiller, Friedrich (1967). *On the Aesthetic Education of Man in a Series of Letters,* ed. Elizabeth M. Wilkinson and L. A. Willoughby. Oxford: Clarendon Press.

Schmitt, Richard (1990). "Murderous Objectivity." In *Thinking the Unthinkable: Meanings of the Holocaust,* ed. Roger Gottlieb. New York: Paulist Press.

———— (1995). *Beyond Separateness: The Relational Nature of Human Beings, Their Autonomy, Knowledge and Power.* Boulder: Westview Press.

———— (2000). *Martin Heidegger on Being Human.* Lincoln: Authors Guild. Available online at Backinprint.com.

Schor, Juliet (2000). *Do Americans Shop Too Much?* Boston: Beacon Press.

Schweickart, David (1993). *Against Capitalism.* New York: Cambridge University Press.

Sebald, W. G. (1996). *The Emigrants.* New York: New Directions.

Sen, Amartya (1999). *Development as Freedom.* New York: Anchor Books.

Sennett, Richard (1998). *The Corrosion of Character: The Personal Consequences of Work in the New Capitalism.* New York: W. W. Norton.

Steptoe, A., G. Fieldman, O. Evans, and L. Perry (1993). "Control over Workplace: Job Strain and Cardiovascular Responses in Middle-Aged Men." *Journal of Hypertension* 11:751–759.

Syfers, James (2000). "Human Rights Versus Classical Liberalism: A Study in the Theory of Value." In *Not for Sale: In Defense of Public Goods*, ed. Anatol Anton, Milton Fisk, and Nancy Holmstrom. Boulder: Westview Press.

Taylor, Charles (1992). *Multiculturalism and the Politics of Recognition*. Princeton: Princeton University Press.

Terkel, Studs (1974). *Working.* New York: Ballantine.

Titmuss, Richard (1971). *The Gift Relationship: From Human Blood to Social Policy.* New York: Vintage.

Tolstoy, Leo (1960). *The Death of Ivan Ilych.* New York: Signet Classic.

Tullock, Gordon, and Richard McKenzie (1985). *The New World of Economics: Explorations into the Human Experience,* 4th ed. Homewoood: Richard Irwin.

Van Parijs, Phillipe (1992). *Arguing for Basic Income: Ethical Foundations for a Radical Reform.* London: Verso.

Wellins, Richard S., William C. Byham, and Jeanne M. Wilson (1991). *Empowered Teams: Creating Self-Directed Work Groups That Improve Quality, Productivity, and Participation.* San Francisco: Jossey-Bass Publishers.

Wenzel, Siegfried (1967). *The Sin of Sloth: Acedia in Medieval Thought and Literature.* Chapel Hill: University of North Carolina Press.

Wickrama, K., R. D. Conger, and F. O. Lorenz (1995). "Work, Marriage, Life Style, and Changes in Men's Physical Health." *Journal of Behavioral Medicine* 18:97–111.

Yates, Richard (1961). *Revolutionary Road.* New York: Bantam.

RECOMMENDED READING

If you want to find more information about some of the topics or authors mentioned in this book, here are some good books to get you started.

Alienation

Bartky, Sandra (1990). "On Psychological Oppression" and "Narcissism, Femininity and Alienation." In Sandra Bartky, *Femininity and Domination*. New York: Routledge.

Finifter, Ada W., ed. (1972). *Alienation and the Social System*. New York: Wiley.

Israel, Joachim (1971). *Alienation from Marx to Modern Sociology*. Boston: Allyn and Bacon.

Marcuse, Herbert (1964). *One-Dimensional Man*. Boston: Beacon Press.

Ollman, Bertell (1971). *Alienation: Marx's Conception of Man in Capitalist Society*. Cambridge: Cambridge University Press.

Schacht, Richard (1970). *Alienation*. New York: Doubleday.

Schmitt, Richard (1983). *Alienation and Class*. Cambridge: Schenckman.

Sennett, Richard (1998). *The Corrosion of Character: The Personal Consequences of Work in the New Capitalism*. New York: Norton.

Rousseau

Cassirer, Ernst (1984). *The Problem Jean-Jacques Rousseau*. New Haven: Yale University Press.

Kierkegaard

Thompson, Josiah (1967). *The Lonely Labyrinth*. Carbondale: Southern Illinois University Press.

Marx

Schmitt, Richard (1997). *Introduction to Marx and Engels: A Critical Reconstruction*. Boulder: Westview Press.

Nietzsche

Danto, Arthur (1965). *Nietzsche as Philosopher.* New York: Macmillan.

Consumer Society

De Graaf, John, David Wann, and Thomas H. Naylor (2001). *Affluenza: The All-Consuming Epidemic.* San Francisco: Barrett-Kohler Publishers.

Wage Work

Terkel, Studs (1974). *Working.* New York: Ballantine.
Sennett, Richard (1998). *The Corrosion of Character: The Personal Consequences of Work in the New Capitalism.* New York: W. W. Norton.

Capitalism and Beyond

Gorz, André (1994). *Capitalism, Socialism, Ecology.* London: Verso.
Schweickart, David (2002). *After Capitalism.* New York: Rowman and Littlefield.

INDEX

Printed in the United States
50331LVS00005B/298